Modern Languages

T0048494

Polity's *Why It Matters* series

In these short and lively books, world-leading thinkers make the case for the importance of their subjects and aim to inspire a new generation of students.

Katrin Kohl

Modern Languages

Why It Matters

polity

The right of Katrin Kohl to be identified as Author of this Work has been asserted in accordance with the UK Copyright, Designs and Patents Act 1988.

First published in 2021 by Polity Press

Polity Press
65 Bridge Street
Cambridge CB2 1UR, UK

Polity Press
101 Station Landing
Suite 300
Medford, MA 02155, USA

ISBN-13: 978-1-5095-4053-2
ISBN-13: 978-1-5095-4054-9 (pb)

A catalogue record for this book is available from the British Library.

Library of Congress Cataloging-in-Publication Data
Names: Kohl, Katrin M. (Katrin Maria), 1956- author.
Title: Modern languages / Katrin Kohl.
Description: Cambridge, UK ; Medford, MA : Polity, 2020. | Series: Why it matters | Includes bibliographical references and index. | Summary: "A star scholar's passionate treatise on how learning other languages can change how we see the world, for the better"-- Provided by publisher.
Identifiers: LCCN 2020033692 (print) | LCCN 2020033693 (ebook) | ISBN 9781509540532 (hardback) | ISBN 9781509540549 (paperback) | ISBN 9781509540556 (epub)
Subjects: LCSH: Languages, Modern--Study and teaching. | Language and languages--Study and teaching--Foreign speakers. | Language and culture.
Classification: LCC PB35 .K64 2020 (print) | LCC PB35 (ebook) | DDC 407.1--dc23
LC record available at https://lccn.loc.gov/2020033692
LC ebook record available at https://lccn.loc.gov/2020033693

Typeset in 11 on 15 Sabon by
Servis Filmsetting Ltd, Stockport, Cheshire
Printed and bound in by Great Britain by CPI Group (UK) Ltd, Croydon

For further information on Polity, visit our website:
politybooks.com

Contents

Preface:
Why Languages Matter

Learning another language unlocks new doors onto the world, and opens doors onto new worlds. It confronts us with different ways of expressing even simple ideas, and enables us to experience ways in which language shapes how we think. Pursuing language learning in the context of studying modern languages develops an understanding of the deep connections between language and culture – and their interdependence.

We all share 'language' – but nobody speaks 'language' as such. It always comes in the form of a particular language that has evolved in a concrete social context. The language with its sounds, words and grammatical structures will have been fashioned by the people who speak it to articulate their kinship relations and hierarchical systems, cultural practices and social concerns, political activities and experiences, trading methods and economic theories, engagement with the local natural world and conception of religious beliefs. That process carries on as we speak – a living language continues to evolve in response to social developments, migration, technical innovation, political pressures and contact with other languages.

Modern languages as a discipline matters in a wide range of ways. Studying one or more languages and the associated cultures opens our minds to different perspectives on the world and different ways of doing things. It immeasurably expands our intellectual horizons and takes us into new worlds of thought and history, literature and art, business practices and political structures. Gaining deep expertise in one or more languages permits immersion in a new context far removed from our comfort zone. It makes travel more rewarding and permits first-hand contact with people from a different culture.

Studying modern languages will always build on the language or languages we know and enrich our understanding of them. Learning a second language opens up the world of language difference. For a student who has grown up with more than one language, familiarity with language difference will form the matrix in which the new language or languages can become embedded. If Urdu or Swahili, Polish or Chinese, Portuguese or Turkish are spoken in the home, this can form a valuable basis for increasing multilingual and multicultural competence, and enhancing appreciation of the value *every* language has in the global conversation.

This book is concerned primarily with languages as an academic discipline and course of study, though much of what is discussed can also apply to language learning more generally. The term 'modern languages' is used here as the generic term for the discipline, though the name can depend on the institutional context. The UK school system, for example, uses 'modern foreign languages'. The designation 'modern' reflects the emergence of the subject in an academic context that was dominated by the 'classical languages' Latin and Greek. Names for degrees vary widely, however – one might follow a degree course in 'Asian languages', or pursue the study of Russian language and culture within the framework of 'Eastern European studies'.

To what extent modern languages constitutes a 'discipline' is a matter of debate, because it is inherently 'interdisciplinary'. Researchers in the field pursue highly diverse projects that might be connected with linguistics, politics, history, literature, film, music, anthropology, gender studies, sociology, refugee studies . . . the list is infinite. What lies at the heart of modern languages, though, is the deep connection between language and culture – language in all its facets, and culture in all its guises. Not language in the abstract, or culture in the abstract, but both together, in a live process of interaction.

While language courses in schools tend to focus mainly on developing language skills, universities offer much more choice. Levels of proficiency may extend from courses for beginners to courses for students with advanced knowledge of the language or languages. 'Languages for all' courses are typically taught in a dedicated language centre in addition to the student's main area of study, which may be in any subject area. In a modern languages degree programme, by contrast, language learning is central to the course, with some degrees combining modern languages with another subject such as history, English literature, philosophy, politics, business studies or a science. Studying for a degree in modern languages involves both learning the practical skills of using one or two (occasionally three) languages, and the study of those languages in their interaction with cultural and social contexts.

Modern languages tends to be understood as a humanities discipline with interdisciplinary reach and often strong connections with social sciences.

Preface

Alongside training practical skills in the language or languages that are being learned, degree courses in modern languages usually include translation, a rich array of options focused on cultural topics, and frequently also historically and politically focused options. Courses normally involve an extended period spent in a country or countries where the language or languages are spoken, offering an immensely enriching opportunity for immersion in the language and culture and potentially for career experience in a new cultural environment.

Students of modern languages may go on to become journalists or teachers, translators or diplomats, interpreters or intelligence officers. Some go into business, others into acting, publishing, law, humanitarian work or conservation. The process of studying one or more languages to degree level brings deep knowledge of one or more languages and their interaction with their cultural contexts, and it develops the ability to learn further languages efficiently. Moreover, it trains a very wide range of 'transferable skills' – a concept that encompasses all the skills honed during the degree course. They range from highly developed powers of analysis and imaginative interpretation through to sophisticated oral and written communication skills. These provide benefits for any career and create opportunities across the whole spectrum of potential jobs.

Whatever the personal interests and educational pathway, the modern linguist will be an important voice in a world which faces challenges that are simultaneously local and global: climate change, migration, social and educational inequality. Addressing such challenges needs people who know why languages matter.

1

Understanding Identity

Our language is our most important means of communication. It enables us to express ourselves, sustains our relationships with our family and friends, empowers us to shape our community and organize our society politically, allows us to conduct trade and create verbal art, and provides us with the means to share our interests and concerns with other groups of people across the globe.

Yet already in this general list, there is an issue about which language achieves all these things. 'My' language is generally fine for talking to the members of my family – though this may not be true if I have parents from different countries or communities. And it may be sufficient for communicating with other members of my society – that will depend on where I live and whether all those people speak the same language as I do. If I live in

1

India, for example, I might need around five languages in my daily interactions with other people. For trade, my language will not be enough if I want to do business with people whose language is different from my own – they will be happy to sell me their products in my language, but if I want to persuade them to buy my products, I will be well advised to engage with them on their terms, in the language they feel most comfortable with. And I will need more than one language to engage with other people across the globe: it is estimated that there are some 6,500–7,000 languages in the world,[1] and while some are gradually dying out as their speakers diminish, others are emerging – an example is Hinglish (a blend of Hindi and English).

Our language, or languages, are fundamental to our personal identity, an intrinsic part of us, deeply embedded in our psyche, and a key force that connects us with our social group. And languages (in the plural) are fundamental to humankind. Research has shown that babies already develop awareness of language difference before they are born.[2] Evidently such awareness is one of our most fundamental life skills, and one we are equipped to develop throughout our lives. As we evolve our sense of self in interaction with our environment, we are continually drawing on, and interacting with, the languages we hear around us. They play a crucial part in making us who we are.

Studying modern languages takes us further on that journey, and it provides a sustained opportunity to discover and explore how deeply a language is connected with the cultural contexts in which it has evolved and to which it contributes. This intrinsic connection is at the heart of why studying modern languages matters.

Divergence and Convergence in the World of Languages

In studying modern languages, the language or languages we know play an important part. Language learning is therefore always a process that enables us to gain an insight into how languages relate to each other: in what ways they are similar, and how they diverge. The differences will always be significant, though if the languages are relatively closely related, we may be able to benefit from similarities in the grammar and from 'cognates': words that historically derive from the same source and have the same or a similar meaning. Approaching a language from English may also give access to English loan words that have entered its vocabulary, for example in the field of electronic media. In negotiating such differences and similarities, we gain first-hand practical experience of two complementary processes that are continually at work in the world of languages: divergence, or growing apart, and convergence, or growing together. Both tendencies have left their multifarious traces in the history of languages.

Globalization, and the increasing importance of technology in our communication practices, can make it seem as if we are all gradually converging on a small number of 'world languages' and indeed that everyone will shortly speak 'global English'. But this would be to misunderstand the role languages play in communication, and to assume that divergence is a thing of the past, with language development being unidirectional so that we might eventually expect all people to speak the same language. In fact, divergence – which we might also think of as diversification, i.e. creating increasing variety – appears to be as universal in languages as convergence.

Already in ancient times, the people who created the myth of the Tower of Babel dreamed of the single 'perfect' language that would allow all human beings to communicate without language barriers and collaborate effortlessly on the project of building a tower tall enough to reach heaven.

They located that language in the past – before God issued the curse of linguistic diversification designed to prevent the people from challenging his power: 'Let us go down, and there confound their language, that they may not understand one another's speech. So the Lord scattered them abroad from thence upon the face of all the earth' (Genesis 11:7–8). The myth will have emerged from everyday experience of the interplay between very local languages and more widespread 'lingua francas' – a Latin term denoting a shared language between groups of people whose local languages are mutually unintelligible. The myth connects linguistic diversification with migration, reflecting an interaction which is a powerful force in globalization today.

In general terms, it would undoubtedly be convenient if everyone spoke the same language. Correspondingly, Polish ophthalmologist Ludwik Lejzer Zamenhof invented Esperanto in the late nineteenth century to establish a universal lingua franca that could be learned easily and would promote peace. As 'conlangs' (constructed languages) go, the experiment was very successful and, on some estimates, there are now two million Esperanto speakers. However, this is a tiny number by comparison with the well over one billion speakers of English and Mandarin respectively, and the over five hundred million speakers each of Hindi and Spanish. What Esperanto lacks is the connection to a particular group identity and tradition that is typical of 'natural' languages, and the political and social power base which is generally associated with languages that become lingua francas, such as Latin in antiquity, French in the seventeenth and eighteenth century, and English, Mandarin, Hindi and Spanish in their various contexts today.

The rise of artificial intelligence also sheds light on the interplay between convergence and divergence in the world of languages. We can now conceive of a world in which communication would be structured around the use of robots and geared to serving useful purposes with the least possible expenditure of resources. It would then be feasible to have only one language – currently probably English – and everyone would have to learn it in order to be able to access the necessities of daily life. But people are different. We are social beings, and we prize our distinctive identities. We evolve and express these through our cultural practices – and our language. The world of AI has recognized this. Developments in AI are converging neither on Robotspeak nor just on English. There is currently also considerable investment in other languages, with companies like Google or Amazon wanting to diversify their language offering far beyond mainstream languages. In the course of this development, there have in fact been reports of chatbots developing a distinctive language in conversation with each other . . .[3]

Cultural Identities and Language Diversity

Studying modern languages as an academic subject provides a sustained opportunity to engage with the role languages play in our own interactions with the world. Rather than analysing this scientifically, as an object of study that is systematically distinguished from subjective experience, modern languages involves adopting a multitude of perspectives, including the subjective experience of learning one or more languages, and using them for practical purposes, social interactions and intellectual exploration. A key part of this process is experiencing a language as special, and coherently different from our own. The unique beauty and expressive power of a language can't be fully appreciated in the abstract, and our unconscious experiences may be as important for perceiving them as what we learn by analysis.

The language or languages we learn at an early age are deeply integrated within our personalities and enable us to 'express ourselves' – a metaphor that is embedded in normal English vocabulary and indicates the important role language plays for our psyche. When engaging with the various people who make up our social context, we are in fact inclined to use multiple 'languages', and to keep switching how we speak or write depending on who we are communicating with. Talking to a brother or sister will never be the same as talking to a teacher or boss. And talking to a baby or dog will differ to a quite extraordinary degree from talking to an adult acquaintance in a formal situation. Differences encompass the choice of words, the grammatical structures, the intonation, the enunciation. A response to a family member may quite adequately just consist of a grunt.

Moreover, in the social groups we are part of, we can see diversification working at all levels. Families share special words, young people speak differently from old people, mathematicians use jargon that is incomprehensible to historians, twins may create a private language. In some families and communities, it is normal to speak two or more mutually unintelligible languages alongside and in interaction with each other. We all belong to many groups simultaneously – a nation, region, city and local community; an ethnic group, age group, social class and gender; a family, friendship group, group of colleagues and interest group. As we participate in distinct but intersecting conversations, we are continually modifying our language habits in subtle ways and adjusting them to accord with the conventions evolved by the respective group.

We might well assume that such communicative complexity is a distinctively human trait. After all, language itself is often said to be what above all distinguishes human beings from other creatures. Certainly it would appear to be the case that some features of human language and language processing are particular to *Homo sapiens*. However, human beings also share aspects of communication with other mammals and indeed birds. One of these is evidently a tendency for groups to develop distinctive language patterns that differentiate them from other groups.

Three examples from species that are not closely related to *Homo sapiens* may elucidate this. A study of sperm whales found that within a group, the sperm whales shared a repertoire of clicks constituting a distinct 'dialect' which differed from that produced by other groups, facilitating group member recognition. A study of young goats discovered that when they were separated into groups, they quickly developed distinct, group-specific 'accents'. Research on yellowhammers – a type of songbird – yielded the finding that a group introduced from Britain to New Zealand in the nineteenth century had preserved its specific 'dialect' rather than adopting the song of other groups in New Zealand.[4] What exactly is meant in each case by 'dialect' or 'accent' is a complex issue. But the general point we can take from these studies is that diversification between groups serves an important function in facilitating and preserving a group's cohesion, and distinguishing it from other groups. This commonality with other species helps to explain why languages are so important for the cultural identity of human beings at all levels of society.

Preserving Linguistic Identities

The importance of language for defining cultural identity can be traced through the methods used to safeguard and preserve it, and these in turn are culturally distinctive because they are grounded in the particular cultural history and practices of the group. Even the process of deciding which language to study – a matter that is likely to be affected, if not predetermined, by what languages are on offer at school or university – is influenced by the historical allegiances and cultural interests of the country in which we receive our education. And the vocabulary of a language is like a storehouse of the group's interactions with other communities, reflecting factors such as geographical proximity, trade, conquests and cultural fashions.

Principles of this kind can be seen at work in dictionaries, which depend on the language being recorded in script. Monolingual dictionaries gather and define the words in current use in the language, while bilingual (or sometimes multilingual) dictionaries give translations of words. Monolingual dictionaries can fulfil an important role in establishing a linguistic identity, and many nation states have given them high status in that context. Such dictionaries create a framework that determines what is part of the vocabulary of the language concerned – and by extension also what is 'outside' it. This makes them on the one hand *descriptive* and on the other hand *normative*. In this dual role, they represent two key principles that can inform our approach to language change.

An example of the tension that can arise between these two principles is a controversy that erupted in 2007 following the publication of a new edition of the *Oxford Junior Dictionary*. A number of words for the natural world, such as *acorn, bluebell, wren* and *pasture*, had been removed, while words referring to electronic media and word processing had been introduced, for example *blog*, *chatroom* and *database*. In 'descriptive' terms, this perfectly accurately reflected changing language needs and usage among young people. In 'normative' terms, however, it raised issues around values and effects. A group of authors argued in an open letter to the publisher that 'reconnecting kids with nature is vital, and needs cultural leadership'. Their chief concern was that children would cease to engage in outdoor activities and that this would negatively affect their health. More recently, nature conservationists have highlighted the need to preserve indigenous names for plants, birds and other animals, arguing that language diversity interacts in important ways with natural diversity.[5] Our language is interconnected with our lives at all levels, and it constitutes an invaluable repository of the environment in which it developed.

The normative power of a dictionary has often been used to define the 'boundaries' of the relevant language, and thereby also the cultural identity of the community. A remarkable project to define a people's linguistic resources was undertaken in the mid-nineteenth century by the Grimm Brothers, as part of their endeavour to establish a German

cultural heritage at a time when the German nation
state was no more than an idea and political aspi-
ration. (Germany was only founded in 1871.)
Alongside collecting fairy tales to preserve and
showcase German folklore – tales that in fact have
complex origins and are read to this day across the
world – they started an ambitious dictionary that
was only completed a hundred years later, in sixteen
volumes. While each word entry in the *Deutsches
Wörterbuch* included copious information about
the history of the word – its etymology – the aim
was not to provide a complete inventory of all the
words in current use among speakers of German.
Instead, a key purpose was to draw a firm boundary around those words which had a 'German'
or 'Germanic' origin and exclude words that had
come from other languages – a policy of exclusion
which even ruled out words such as *Adresse* and
demokratisch, which Jacob Grimm used himself.[6]
To this day, words used widely in German such as
Mikrofon or *Jeans* are termed *Fremdwörter* (foreign
words), even though current German is inconceiv-
able without words borrowed especially from Latin
and increasingly from English.

In France, the preservation of French cultural
identity through linguistic curation has a much more
continuous institutional history in the form of the

Académie Française, or French Academy (see Figure 1). This was established by royal decree in 1635 as the official national authority regulating all matters concerning the French language. While it now has no legal status, its normative pronouncements continue to have considerable authority, enshrined in the motto *À l'immortalité* (To immortality). Its forty members – dubbed *les immortels* (the immortals) – are in charge of the official dictionary of French, which remains the most traditional dictionary of the French language, with borrowings from other languages and new technical words being introduced only very cautiously. In 2008, the Academy objected to recognition of regional languages in the French constitution on the grounds that this would be an 'attack on national identity' and that it would go against the constitutionally established primary role of (standard) French: 'Depuis plus de cinq siècles, la langue française a forgé la France' (For over five centuries, the French language has forged France).[7] The nation's language is here claimed to have moulded the nation into a culturally coherent whole.

French became the main language of diplomacy in the seventeenth century and retained that status until the twentieth century. It continues to have a key role in international institutions and, as a tool

Figure 1. The architectural image on the cover of the French dictionary published by the Académie Française asserts its role as the institutional guardian of the French language. (Bodleian Library, Oxford)

15

of soft power, in France's erstwhile colonial sphere of influence. This in turn prompts more general questions about the historical factors and current mechanisms that make particular languages into powerful tools of cultural, political and financial dominance.

Languages as a Political Minefield

The role of languages in defining cultural identity has always given them a political dimension. But this plays out in very different ways depending on the status of the language in its particular context and the role of the speakers, or users, of that language. A crucial part of studying modern languages is understanding language hierarchies, what underpins them, and why they need to be questioned and dismantled. Language difference all too often translates into exclusion of 'other' languages. The fact that a language has a larger number of speakers is frequently seen as a mark of superior educational importance. And the communicative benefits of sharing a lingua franca are often confused with that language's supposedly superior value.

Hierarchical constructions of the relationships between languages are inextricably connected with political and economic inequalities. This can readily be seen in the traditional and enduring predominance of the languages exported by colonial powers to other parts of the world in processes of violent conquest and often obliteration of indigenous communities and their cultures and languages. For modern languages, the project of decolonizing the syllabus therefore has special resonance because it goes to the heart of the subject: the languages offered for study tend to be languages that gained dominance by means of colonial conquest. The urgency injected by the #BlackLivesMatter movement has highlighted the dearth of courses available for learning African languages. And it acts as a powerful reminder that modern languages is a discipline with a responsibility: to promote not just the value of supposedly 'major' languages but the value of *all* languages.[8]

Even where multiculturalism is embraced, this does not necessarily entail that languages which form part of the cultural diversity are respected, or that their speakers are given the opportunity to develop them educationally. Much work needs to be done to make the diversity of languages within our societies more visible and strengthen the perceived value of those languages. Each and every one has emerged as a unique communicative medium from a particular place and in a particular historical context, and each one forms an important bridge to other parts of the world, via its speakers.

For speakers of English as a first language living in an anglophone country, language diversity may collapse simply into 'English' versus 'foreign', though different parts of a country may show very different patterns of language use, often depending largely on past or recent migration. For example, Spanish is the main language spoken at home for around 12.6% of people in the United States,[9] but the percentage is very much higher in the western states and very much lower in the eastern ones. And half of all residents in some major urban areas of the United States speak a language other than English at home, while in other areas, English is typically the language of the home as well as the language of public life. The degree of tolerance towards linguistic difference will tend to vary, and can be affected by political shifts. In the United Kingdom, for example, the decision to leave the European Union taken in 2016 and implemented in 2020 arguably resulted in increased 'linguaphobia' (fear of foreign languages) in some parts of the population. In Germany, debates concerning immigration around the year 2000 involved discussion of the concept of a German *Leitkultur* (lead culture), with a requirement for immigrants to learn German and assimilate culturally. In such scenarios, the language of the majority holds sway and can become a means of suppressing plurality.

A language can attain particular political sensitivity in repressive regimes that seek to enforce use of an official language as a means of stamping out an independent cultural identity and potential political challenge. Such a strategy was evident in fascist Spain, when General Franco established Spanish as the only official language in 1939. In Catalonia, for example, the use of Catalan – which had been permitted during the Second Spanish Republic from 1931 to 1939 – was banned throughout the Franco era in public administrative contexts and in schools. From 1975, this history of suppression enhanced the status of the language as a means of articulating political autonomy, a role Catalan has retained in the independence movement of Catalonia.

The political value ascribed to their language by cultural minorities demonstrates that people don't simply settle for the most convenient language if this conflicts with their desire for culturally distinctive self-expression. In the United Kingdom, language plays an important role in defining the cultural identities of the three smaller nations, Scotland, Wales and Northern Ireland, with Wales having pursued by far the most rigorous and unified language policy. A concerted strategy of language revival has meant that Wales is now a fully functioning bilingual country. The Welsh government invests significant funding in bilingual policy documentation, education and public signage, and many families choose schools in which Welsh is the first language. These were established from 1956 in order to preserve Welsh and embed it firmly as a living language for the long term. Public support for the first-language education policy is sustained by a passionate commitment to Welsh musical and poetic culture, which finds regular expression in national, regional and local *eisteddfods* – competitive festivals of poetry and music that are fashioned as a celebration of the bardic tradition (see Figure 2). As in Catalonia, a distinct linguistic heritage interacts with a distinct political identity.

The social and political effect of linguistic distinctiveness is evident whenever we hear people speaking a language amongst themselves that is unfamiliar to us: we experience it as 'different', 'foreign' or indeed 'alien'. Language learning enables us to develop a more nuanced approach to linguistic difference. In making the effort to bridge the gap between our own language and another, and in gradually gaining understanding of the other language as connected to

Figure 2. The annual National Eisteddfod of Wales culminates in the Chairing of the Bard. Shown here is Gruffudd Eifion Owen, who won the Chair in 2018. The ceremony is presided over by the Archdruid, who asks the crowd, 'A oes heddwch?' (Is there peace?). The crowd answers 'Heddwch!', and the sword is therefore not fully pulled out of its sheath.

© EGC/Aled Llywelyn

our own by patterns of similarity and divergence, we overcome our distrust and embrace the difference. Studying modern languages – *any* language and its cultural dimension – enables us to understand how vitally distinctive languages contribute to our individual lives as social beings.

2

Experimenting with a New Medium

Learning a language is like entering a different way of thinking, feeling and living. Every aspect of language may play a part in this process. Studying modern languages is useful in expanding our communicative options and social interactions in a multilingual world. But it matters far beyond that. Moving around in a new communicative medium makes us continually aware of the creative potential within our daily language use. In grappling with how another language works, we keep on discovering new perspectives on our own language, and start exploring the linguistic processes we have learned over a lifetime in new contexts.

A single word referring to a practical everyday occurrence in another language can evoke associations that are not fully replicable in our own and get us thinking about the extraordinary potential that words have to shape our concepts and direct our thoughts. An example is the German word *Feierabend*, formed by joining up *Feier* (celebration) with *Abend* (evening). The compound noun – in use at least since the seventeenth century – can mean both the end of the working day, as in *Feierabend machen* (to finish work), and the leisure time after the end of work, as in *den Feierabend genießen* (to enjoy one's evening after work). The rich opportunities German offers for building compound nouns here generate a distinctive concept that is more than the sum of its parts – marking both the temporal point of transition and the period afterwards. By contrast with an equivalent English expression, the word invests the time period after work with positive emotional value and, as it were, protected status. This in turn makes it into a thing with focused political potential: Works Councils have used the concept rhetorically in campaigns to defend workers against having to deal with emails and phone calls after work: 'Rettet den Feierabend' (Save the evening leisure time).[1] The difference by comparison with English is subtle, but it extends beyond superficial form into emotional, cultural and political reality.

Modern languages is a discipline that encompasses both 'the medium' and 'the message', both 'language' and 'content', and the multifarious ways in which they intersect. By contrast with studying linguistics, which analyses language and languages primarily as objects of scientific investigation, studying modern languages involves immersion in active practice: speaking and listening, reading and writing, experiencing how a language works and interacts with the cultures that form part of its history and fabric. Linguistics may form part of the study of modern languages, providing insight into ways in which general linguistic patterns manifest themselves in the specific language, and with sociolinguistics in particular shedding important light on its use. But at the centre of the discipline of modern languages is the process of developing a deep understanding of one or more languages as they manifest themselves in practice, in their cultural contexts.

Tapping into Creative Potential

Our ability to communicate with each other through language is one of our most powerful talents, and it is a skill we carry on perfecting throughout our lives. We hear one or more languages before we are even born, and learn at least one language from the people around us. The language or languages we grow up with help to shape how we think, provide the key instrument for our interaction with other members of the society we grow up in, and are central to our unique personal identity. As members of our language community, we create language as we use it. A simple test can reveal the creative work that is involved in our individual routine use of language. If you type a sentence of some twelve words into your browser (enclosed by double quotation marks to make it search only for the identical string), you will be likely to discover that it is not replicated anywhere else on the internet – you can reduce the string to see at what point you find that other people have used the same sequence of words. At the level of single words, too, language communities are enormously creative, and individuals both contribute and respond to this ongoing creative energy. Communities are continually inventing new words and meanings that quickly become part of the shared vocabulary – this is evident in the words associated with social media created in the early part of the twenty-first century, such as 'tweet', 'trending', 'hashtag' or 'emoji'.

These creative, experimental learning capabilities that are built into the daily use of our own language are available for learning new languages as well, and it's worth opening up spaces for connecting with that creative energy as we learn. Depending on individual habits and preferences, these can take the form of writing poetry or short prose pieces, which might be all in the new language or bilingual. They might also include nonsense sounds and words. Playing with language is an important part of human language use, as David Crystal has shown for English in his book *Language Play* (1998).[2] When learning a language, playing with its elements allows the new words, sounds and grammatical structures to become more freely embedded in our linguistic repertoire, connecting up productively with our existing linguistic resources.

Writing a diary – however short and ad hoc – can also be a great way to experiment with the language in a mental and emotional space that is free from the angst of getting things wrong. It can offer a place to record intriguing discoveries in a mixture of one's own language and the language being learned, note funny 'false friends' such as English 'embarrassed' versus Spanish *embarazada* (pregnant), or reflect on an embarrassing mistake made in a class. Exploring the language history of one's own family and the different regional variations contributed by family members can form a theme, as can explorations of names for favourite dishes in different languages. Writing a personal diary can fruitfully complement reading about other people's language journeys, for example in the collection *How Languages Changed My Life* (2019).[3] An extended language memoir can make stimulating reading in the process of learning a language oneself. A landmark in this genre is *In altre parole/In Other Words* (2015/2016) by Pulitzer Prize-winning American author Jhumpa Lahiri.[4] Born in London and growing up speaking Bengali in the home, she became fascinated with Italian when visiting Florence after college and eventually decided to relocate to Italy with her husband and children in order to immerse herself in the language. The book charting her linguistic experiment is written by herself in Italian, with an English version produced by a translator on the facing pages. It is a very personal story, taking the reader on an ambitious journey into another mental and cultural world – a world Lahiri wished to remain in as she wrote about finding her creative voice in the language she had only learned as an adult.

Doing a short, practically focused course in a new language provides a glimpse of how different it feels to step out of a linguistic framework which is so familiar that we don't even notice it is there. Conversely for some people, moving between two languages is second nature. But there's nothing quite like studying a foreign language intensively over a long period of time, and immersion through living in a country where it's spoken everywhere, all the time. Part of that process is finding out how people tick who experience that language as intrinsically connected with their culture and their heritage. The practical business of learning a language is also a commitment to exploring new mental pathways. And if we wake up one morning and find that we have been dreaming in that language and it no longer feels foreign, it has become part of who we are – a medium for discovering a whole new way of being oneself, and being part of a new community.

Everyone's a Linguist

Some people grow up with more than one language in their lives – perhaps a 'heritage' language is spoken in the home that differs from the main language of the country, or the grandparents live in a different country. The local community or the school may include people who speak different languages. Such diversity is always a valuable opportunity for extending one's experience of languages, and this can indeed open up career advantages as well as enriching personal life and relationships.[5]

Bilingualism and multilingualism haven't always been considered an advantage, however. Until quite recently, and to some extent even today in countries that see themselves as monolingual, there has been a view that children 'naturally' speak one language, and that knowledge of this language is impaired by adding another. Neuroscientific research has turned that view on its head. It now seems likely that there are more bilingual and multilingual speakers in the world than monolinguals.[6] And for the brain, using more than one language appears to be beneficial, and rather similar to the use of muscles – 'use it or lose it'. Studies suggest that in bilingual and multilingual people, the onset of symptoms of dementia is typically delayed by some four years in comparison with monolinguals. Moreover, equivalent benefits are found for people who learn languages.[7]

There is also a more general question that arises from the burgeoning interest in bilingualism and multilingualism: is *anyone* actually 'monolingual', and if so, what does that mean? Consider all the aspects of language in which we are continually selecting from a wide range of possibilities. To take just one example, here is a range of English expressions you can use when parting from someone: *farewell, goodbye, bye-bye, bye, cheerio, cheers, adieu, au revoir, ciao, adios, toodle-oo, toodle-pip, good night*, *night-night*, *all the best*, *have a nice day*, *see you later*, *in a bit*, *see you around*, *be seeing you*, *see you*, *see ya*, *so long*, *God bless*, *look after yourself*, *take care*. It could be objected that *au revoir*, *ciao* and *adios* are French, Italian and Spanish respectively – but they have made it into the *Oxford English Dictionary*. *Adieu* would seem extraordinarily antiquated – or amusingly ironic. Moreover, there will be many further options that are regionally specific, or specific to particular communities. They're worth listening out for – a touch of multilingualism in our midst.

Committing to a Language

If we bear in mind that there are some seven thousand languages one might theoretically learn (see above, p. 2), modern languages is an academic subject like no other, since it entails an extraordinary degree of specialization early on. It is rather like learning a musical instrument: if I want to get to a level of competence that enables me to play great music, I will fairly quickly need to decide on the one or two instruments to which I will commit serious time.

Different languages allow us to access different cultures. We may feel particularly drawn to the sounds of a certain language or to the cultural world in which a language is embedded. When deciding on a language to study at degree level, one option can be to carry on a language learned at school and develop it further. If a learner makes good progress early on and enjoys the language, it makes a lot of sense to deepen and extend that knowledge, find out more about the communities in which it is spoken, visit a country where it is the main language, read books, watch films and follow news reports in the language.

On the other hand, some people choose to study a language for reasons that are uniquely personal – perhaps a grandparent speaks the language, or they have spent a holiday or part of their life in a country where it is spoken. Then again, one might choose a language on the basis of its being particularly well suited to a career interest. In practice, the range of languages offered even at university level is limited, with courses that may speak to some people's interests more than others. Before embarking on a course, it is important to research what languages are available, how they are taught, and what type of cultural content the available courses focus on. Ultimately, though, every language is worth learning. It puts us in touch with new people, enables us to explore exciting places and fresh ideas, and opens up a new part of the world that will always be rewarding to explore.

The analogy of learning a musical instrument is also useful for considering how to approach the process of learning a language. Key principles are that it will inevitably involve hard work, that it needs to be sustained over a long time, and that it is important not to set the bar too high with respect to the rate of progress.

Learning a language comes naturally to children – though anyone who observes a child learn their first language will notice how much experimentation, practice and repetition it involves, and how much input from people around them. Children will also learn further languages relatively easily, especially if there is a pressing need, perhaps because the child has moved to a different country.

In later life, languages are mostly learned in less helpful circumstances: generally in the context where our first language is spoken all around us, so the motivation to communicate in the new language has to be generated artificially; during a tiny proportion of the week; in a class of other learners so each person gets very little individual practice; with classroom tasks that may be experienced as stressful because one is afraid of making mistakes and coming across to the class as stupid; or at a time of day when one is rather tired. Moreover, progress tends to be very slow, so it's easy to get discouraged, lose motivation and assume one is no good at languages. In fact, anglophone countries are full of people who think they have no talent for languages – a common self-assessment is that 'Languages are not my thing'.

The fact is that we tend to have unrealistic expectations about the speed of progress – after all, we learned our own language in a way that we remember as effortless. Yet even for children, it takes a very long time to learn a language well and acquire the ability to use it proficiently. It has been estimated that they spend on average around 9,000 hours learning their first language by the time they reach the age of five.[8] How long it takes to learn a language as a teenager or adult depends enormously on circumstances, and it needs to be factored in that learning a language outside a country where it is normally spoken happens alongside many other commitments. Moreover, learners differ enormously, and respond very differently to the challenges of learning vocabulary, understanding and using grammatical rules, listening, oral production, reading and writing. By comparison with learning a language earlier on, however, we can benefit from learning strategies acquired in the course of our general learning career, and develop new ones suited to language learning. These can significantly speed up progress.

Language learning apps can be very helpful, especially in the early stages and even with advanced vocabulary learning, not least because they allow the individual learner to personalize the rate of progress. Learning together with other people can inject fun and a stimulating element of competition. Important principles are not to expect too much of yourself, and to keep going, doing a little and often.

Ultimately, there is no one-size-fits-all best solution to learning a language. This isn't really surprising. Learning a language interacts with who we are, with our personal learning style and with our personal circumstances and degree of motivation. The more we connect the new language with the immensely complex knowledge of language we already have, and the deeply familiar skills we have mastered of speaking and listening, reading and writing, the more effective and enjoyable the learning process will be. And the more we are able to integrate our language learning with our other interests, the more likely it is that we will sustain our motivation and carry on with the learning process.

Systematically pursuing a personal interest through the language being studied can form a central part of a degree course, connect with it, or complement it. It might be an interest in an author, computer games, daily news, theatre, pop music, cooking, football, medieval castles, travel or a political movement. Delving deep into that area and finding out all about it through the medium of the language and in the context of the cultures associated with the language provides an entry route into a rich world that will be populated with many other people who share that interest. It also opens up a historical trajectory, for there is no aspect of culture that doesn't have roots going back into the past. To learn a language, it isn't necessary to be a language nerd. But it can be helpful to develop obsessive enthusiasm in some area of one's life and give it a new, language-rich dimension.

The Infinite Potential of Transferable Skills

The combination of practical and theoretical processes involved in modern languages opens up a wide range of pathways towards enriching 'transferable skills', especially when language study is pursued simultaneously with studying the cultural contexts in which the language is used – as a medium of communication, as a means of expressing emotions, as a source of art.

The concept of transferable skills is employment-speak for all those skills we learn in the course of education (and life) that are of a more general kind than subject knowledge, such as adaptability, resilience, team-working and time management. The concept is worth thinking about because it highlights the fact that, in studying a subject, we are stretching our mind and expanding our skill-set at the same time as acquiring subject-specific knowledge. These benefits will typically overlap with those acquired in other degree courses, but they will nevertheless gain a special twist from the particular course of study. So what special benefits do modern languages offer us? It trains cognitive skills – both those that are typical of the humanities and to some extent social sciences, and those developed by systematic language learning and use, including communication skills. It also strengthens social confidence since language learning continually confronts the learner with the need to perform. If we follow the language to the countries where it is spoken, it can enhance our adaptability and cultural understanding. And all of this together is ideally suited to enabling us to think outside the box – invaluable for both life and work.

Studying modern languages at degree level typically involves a year or a semester spent in a country where the language is spoken. Whether it's spent doing one or more internships, teaching English in a school, or attending university, it's a marvellous opportunity to experience an extended period of time simultaneously working on the language in the most effective way possible and gaining experience of living in a country other than one's own with enough knowledge of the language and culture to gain a sense of 'belonging'. Starting any new course or job is challenging, but doing so in a new cultural context, in a language other than one's own, in a place where one doesn't know anyone, involves a big leap out of the personal comfort zone. Perhaps a job needs to be found, and somewhere to live. There are new people to get to know, new conventions to discover – sometimes the hard way, by making mistakes – and unfamiliar administrative procedures to negotiate.[9] There's nothing quite like this to train all manner of transferable skills – life skills and work skills.

It is also worth devoting thought to how studying languages in interaction with their cultural contexts enhances communication skills. This question keys into the whole range of what the ancient Greeks and Romans developed into the art of rhetoric. Rhetoric covered the entire process of preparing a speech to suit the audience and purpose: identifying relevant ideas and arguments; structuring them in a meaningful and effective sequence; crafting the style; designing the gestures and body language to strengthen the effect of the words; and committing the speech to memory so it could be delivered with spontaneity and conviction. Ultimately, training a rhetorician was an all-encompassing educational programme, since persuasive public speaking extended to all subjects under the sun and was valuable in all walks of life. The ancient art of rhetoric embodies a profound confidence in the power of language, and the need to attend to its role in society.

Studying modern languages is similarly broadly based, and effective in training communication skills as part of a bigger concern to engage with society in all its facets. Extending our communicative competence into a new linguistic medium not only opens up a whole new communicative arena. It also immeasurably expands our appreciation of the crucial role communication must play in promoting social cohesion and intercultural understanding.

A multitude of careers require such skills, and it's worth putting research early on into the question of what careers are available, which ones appeal, and what they require. A wide range of international organizations – the EU and the UN, diplomatic services and intelligence agencies, trade missions,

NGOs and corporations – require highly qualified linguists with sophisticated cultural awareness, and they will often provide opportunities for further, more specialized language training. Other career paths may draw less on language and subject-specific skills and more on the generic, transferable skills acquired in the course of study. Communication will always be key.

Effective intercultural communication is more important than ever, both in the international context of globalization and within our diverse societies. It works best when it is a two-way process, when *both* sides are sensitive to the implications and effects of cultural difference, and when *both* sides engage in dialogue to explore the common ground. Committing to language learning and an understanding of cultural contexts is invaluable in fostering an open-minded willingness to engage with perspectives other than our own.

3

Exploring Difference

Modern languages is a discipline that moves across borders, continually training an ability to understand and appreciate difference while also building bridges and revealing richly populated borderlands where languages and cultures meet and mingle. First and foremost, it confronts us on a daily basis with the many differences between the language or languages we know, and the language or languages we are learning. Meanwhile it also gives us new insights into our own language, inviting us to see its vocabulary, its grammar and the way its sounds relate to its script in new ways. The fruitfulness of comparative work between one's own language and the language being learned is highlighted in a statement by the German writer and polymath Goethe: 'Wer fremde Sprachen nicht kennt, weiß nichts von seiner eigenen' (A person who does not know foreign languages, knows nothing about their own).[1]

Bilingual and multilingual communities routinely experience language difference in the daily process of communicating with people. Negotiating it involves moving between points of view, and seeing difference not as a threat but as a key part of human life. Intriguingly, research indeed suggests that bilinguals are better at conflict resolution than monolinguals.[2] Movement across languages can take many forms, and bilingual or multilingual communities will engage in it all the time. It may consist of code-switching or translanguaging, when a speaker mixes elements from different languages, for example starting a sentence in one and completing it in another, or including expressions from one language in an utterance made in another. This will be most usual where the speakers involved in the conversation are all familiar with both languages. Other forms are interpreting, a term used for transfer from one language to another in oral discourse, and translation, which involves transfer from a piece of written text in one language to a text in another language. The focus in this chapter is on translation and the ways in which it can sharpen our understanding of how languages differ. This in turn offers deep insight into the ways in which meaning is created through language.

Over the last couple of decades, it has come to seem as if translation is becoming less and less dependent on human skills and may soon be wholly automated. Machine translation has improved to the point where it may produce a perfectly acceptable translation for information purposes. So what is the point of engaging with translation, which is often an important part of a modern languages course? A careers-focused answer might argue that even sophisticated software using a big corpus of textual examples may produce workable versions of straightforward texts, but it won't supply the context-specific, culturally intelligent interpretation that is a vital aspect of translation. This can apply as much to a letter from a CEO to shareholders as to a work of philosophy or a novel. There is, however, also another dimension that gives translation high value when studying modern languages: no other language activity takes us so deeply into experiencing the nature of language difference as the practice of translation.

Umberto Eco – author of the novel *Il nome della rosa* (1980, The Name of the Rose) and stimulating commentator on the practice, art and theory of translation – states in his book *Mouse or Rat? Translation as Negotiation* (2003) that 'translation is always a shift, not between two languages but between two cultures'.[3] While the basic point is important, it doesn't take account of the live interaction between language and culture. The premise here is rather that translation involves a shift simultaneously between languages and between cultures. Moreover, the process of shifting opens up a text to new readings and often multiple new contexts.

Untranslatable Words?

A fascinating starting point for looking at what is at stake in translation are the many websites listing 'untranslatable words'. The items they list generally give an insight into a culturally rich concept that is embodied in a single, culturally distinctive word: Spanish *sobremesa* – the time spent chatting at the table after the meal is finished; or Russian *toska* – pining, spiritual anguish, aching of the soul, nostalgia. It's not that these words can't be translated by paraphrase. But the single word fuses a range of associations into an organic whole, allowing them to lie dormant or be activated depending on the context, and generating for speakers of the language an immediate rich understanding of the whole that is not just cerebral but visceral.

So *are* such words 'untranslatable'? And if so, where is the boundary between translatable and untranslatable words? Taking Spanish and English as an example, the physical world yields many straightforwardly translatable words, for example *brazo* (arm), *piedra* (stone) or *mesa* (table). Bilingual dictionaries with their word-for-word translations seem to support the view that translatability is the norm – though larger dictionaries list contexts and phrases for a given entry which indicate that translation is context-dependent. Ultimately, a binary distinction between translatable and untranslatable words would presuppose that the Spanish and English lexical systems – that is, the way their vocabulary is organized – are in principle identical and that we should normally find a word in the English system in an equivalent 'place' to the one it occupies in the Spanish system. Where Spanish has the word *sobremesa*, we should expect to find an English equivalent, but since there is a cultural 'gap' given different mealtime practices in anglophone countries, the 'untranslatable' Spanish word has to be paraphrased.

This would, however, be to ignore the nature of lexical systems. For the words of a language don't gain their meaning and use from a 'real' connection with real objects that is essentially replicated in every language in the same way. Rather, words are signs that are in themselves arbitrary and gain meaning from their place in the specific language's lexical system. That system and the words and expressions within it are continually on the move as words evolve in response to changing contexts, new words come into the language, existing ones subtly shift their meaning or add new ones, and words or meanings become obsolete.

These processes are evident in the wealth of words that have emerged to refer to electronic media, or been repurposed, such as 'internet', 'web' or 'mouse'. An example can be traced in the responses in different languages to the words 'network' in the field of computing and electronic media, with derivations such as 'to network' and 'social networking'. For example, French has extended the metaphorical uses of the existing noun *réseau* (network), which has long been used for systems such as a 'railway network' or 'spy network', and coupled it with common verbs, for example *travailler en réseau* (to work as a network), while also expressing the idea in a different way, for example *prendre des contacts*. German speakers have similarly drawn on the existing noun *Netzwerk* but created the verb *netzwerken* (with the past participle *genetzwerkt*) for the process of networking. Additionally, they have borrowed from English to create *networken*, with the past participle *genetworkt* or *genetworked*. The Germanic form has gained more traction, probably because it is in any case close to the English word while being readily integrated in the German lexical system – but the loan word can win out to add a touch of cool.

The solutions found in these languages are not simply a matter of chance. That there is a pattern can be seen with the English verb 'to google' as a term for searching the internet – formed from the trademark of the most widely used search engine. In Romance languages, the name of the search engine is typically combined with a standard verb, with some variability in the connecting preposition, for example French *chercher sur/avec Google*, Spanish *buscar con/en Google* and Italian *cercare con/in Google*. German has by contrast followed in the footsteps of English, only changing the spelling to add an established German verb ending when creating *googeln* with the past participle *gegoogelt*. These examples give a glimpse of ways in which individual languages evolve – responding to things in the world and human ideas; exploiting historically rooted patterns of word formation offered by the language; drawing on other languages; and

46

reflecting preferences of the language's speakers. Translation simultaneously forms a dynamic part of that process and responds to it creatively.

Rather than distinguishing between 'translatable' and 'untranslatable' words and expressions, it is therefore more fruitful in principle to envisage translation as a process of mediating between two different language systems, each of which interacts with a multiplicity of cultural contexts. Finding a suitable translation may involve a straightforward equivalent but it will often require more complex choices based on interpretation. This in turn requires understanding both the context the text originated in and the context(s) for which the translation is intended. Language systems are fluid, and a translation is always more than the sum of its parts.

Translating Nuggets of Cultural History

A fun part of learning a language, and translation from and into it, is the role of idioms and sayings. They may reflect general worldly wisdom, and they may give us little scenarios that take us back to a world that has receded into the past but remains alive in the community's everyday speech. They can yield surprising similarities across two languages, or be wonderfully challenging to translate when they require a leap of the imagination. They normally play a small part in translation but they can tell us a lot about the metaphorical dimension of translation more generally, and also shed light on the question of 'literal' versus 'free' translation.

With metaphorical idioms, it makes sense to distinguish between the 'literal' meaning of the individual words and the metaphorical meaning of the whole phrase. For example, the French idiom *Ce n'est pas la mer à boire* could be translated literally as 'That's not the sea to drink' or 'You don't have to drink the sea' – but this wouldn't convey the same point in English as in French, where the expression is a stock phrase that is used metaphorically. Suitable translations, depending on context and translator choice, might be 'We're not asking the impossible', 'It's not asking too much', 'It's not a big deal' or perhaps 'It surely isn't such a big deal, is it?' With an idiom of this kind, used conventionally as a chunk, one can justifiably say that while the 'literal' word-for-word translation is incorrect, a rendering that conveys the meaning of the whole is not 'free' – it is appropriate.

The translation of such an idiom gives us an insight into the fact that translation is always mediating between two language systems, not isolated bits of them. The systems differ not just in their individual words, but also in the configuration of the verbal and syntactic units by which they express things. The concept of 'literal' versus 'free' translation may be a convenient binary shorthand to indicate the difference between two translations, but it risks distorting how translation – and indeed language – works.

Like many idioms and sayings, *Ce n'est pas la mer à boire* draws on an element of the natural world to make a general point, connecting it with a bodily action. While this example is timeless, others are firmly embedded in a cultural context, sometimes contexts that have ceased to be relevant to current living conditions or lifestyles. Examples in English are 'Make hay while the sun shines' or 'Go on a wild goose chase'. While the former gains its meaning from farming practice that is no longer familiar to most English speakers, the latter presupposes catching animals for food oneself rather than procuring prepared meat from a shop. They constitute a culturally rich link with past contexts that have contributed to making the language what it is today.

Especially where the practices have ceased to be part of everyday life, the idioms and sayings mark moments of interaction between language and culture, offering glimpses of how the language of a cultural group connects individual speakers to the group's cultural past. An example is the German expression *Kleinvieh macht auch Mist.* Translated literally, it means 'Small livestock also produces dung'. Whereas the English equivalent stock phrase 'Every little helps' is culturally neutral, the German saying harks back to an era when people kept domestic animals, and manure was a valuable commodity for cultivating the land. Both the cultural practice and the value system it embodies have receded into the past, but they have left a trace in the language, rather like a little root connecting the individual speaker to earlier generations who spoke the language and used it to articulate their daily experience of keeping livestock.

Such roots subtly sustain our link with the heritage of the community we form part of. This is not a dimension that readily lends itself to translation. Identifying that dimension in the language of the text, and interpreting the function of the idiom in its textual context, is an important part of translation, forming the basis for finding an appropriate alternative form of expression.

Idioms and sayings of this kind in effect evoke a tiny scenario that gives concrete shape to an abstract meaning. In some cases, the specific cultural context in which the expression arose is key to understanding the meaning. Take this Spanish idiom: *dar la vuelta a la tortilla*. It literally means 'to turn over the tortilla' and you might find it in a recipe. So what type of *tortilla* is it referring to? The 'small' Spanish *torta* (cake) – the ending *-illa* signals small size – made of eggs and often containing fried potatoes, other vegetables or pieces of sausage? Or the Mexican flatbread made from corn flour and used for wraps – originally called *tlaxcalli* by the indigenous Nahuatl speakers and named *tortilla* by the Spanish colonizers in the sixteenth century? The former is right – the relevant *tortilla* is what is often known as 'Spanish omelette' in English (which borrowed the French word when a similar type of egg dish came to Britain from France). But being an idiom, the phrase has a meaning that goes beyond the literal: metaphorically, it means 'to turn round a situation' – normally for the better. It is a brilliantly vivid way of using an everyday physical action carried out with food to convey the act of bringing about radical change. The expression is both specific to the Spanish language and embedded in the food culture of Spain.

There is a real loss when such a culturally rich idiom has to be translated into another language where the equivalent is perfectly serviceable but rather dull. It offers scope for the translator's creativity in finding an equally effective equivalent idiom, or compensating for the loss with an alternative culturally rich contribution to the text. Experiencing that sense of cultural loss in the process of translation is, however, valuable, for it tells us something fundamental about why people care so deeply about 'their' language. It is the lifeblood of their community and its heritage, and it connects them with the communicative medium in which they have grown up – the richest instrument for expressing their emotional, intellectual and social identity. In a very real sense, a culturally rich idiom is a bit of 'home' inside us.

The Past and Future of Translation

We can assume that interpreting, in the sense of converting orally what a person says from one language into another, has existed ever since human languages came into being. Translation, in the sense of transforming a text written in one language into a text written in another, is more recent, and emerged as languages were recorded in written form. A sophisticated example is the Rosetta Stone, created in Memphis in Egypt in 196 BCE (see Figure 3a). It issues a decree establishing the religious cult of the newly crowned Pharaoh

Figure 3a. The Rosetta Stone, with a decree passed by a council of priests affirming the royal cult of the thirteen-year-old Ptolemy V on the first anniversary of his coronation in 196 BCE.

Ptolemy V in three versions, two of them forms of Egyptian (in hieroglyphs, see Figure 3b, and in Demotic script) and one ancient Greek (in the Greek alphabet, see Figure 3c). The discovery that all three texts conveyed the same content was invaluable in that it permitted Egyptian hieroglyphs to be deciphered.

It isn't just chance that the word 'interpreting' is identical to the word we use for understanding and explaining meaning within a language: the meaning of an action undertaken by others that is ambiguous in its intent, or the meaning of what someone says that is not immediately transparent, or the meaning of a piece of text such as a poem. 'Interpreting' in those senses takes place without negotiating a difference between two languages. It can be envisaged as finding common ground between two participants: meaning produced by the creator of the action, utterance or text, and meaning created by the recipient on the basis of the action, utterance or text. 'Interpreting' in the sense of oral translation between languages is a particular form of that same process, involving the distinctive aspect that it involves two mutually unintelligible languages. If we come to this from a monolingual context, it seems like a very different matter from other forms of interpretation. However, from a multilingual

Figure 3b. Inscription in hieroglyphs, including a cartouche with the name Ptolemy, written right to left together with an Egyptian honorific.

Figure 3c. Inscription in ancient Greek, including the name Ptolemy: ΠΤΟΛΕΜΑΙΟΣ.

perspective, it is part of a continuum of intercultural and interpersonal exchange.

One might say that little changed in principle between the processes of interpreting and translation people engaged in during the era of the Rosetta Stone, and the activity carried out by interpreters and translators up until the end of the twentieth century. In both cases, the act of converting an utterance or text from one language into another was carried out by a human being. This is still the case for most interpreting and also for many types of translation, even though translators now increasingly draw on corpus-based electronic resources such as Linguee.com for widely used languages such as English, French, Spanish or German. However, the advent of machine translation and – more slowly – machine interpretation, and their rapid refinement using ever bigger electronic text corpora, have brought a sea change that in effect marks the industrialization and automation of that conversion process all in one go.

To get a sense of the scale of the change, one might envisage the conversion of a text the size of the King James Bible, which took forty-seven biblical scholars some seven years to complete in the early seventeenth century, being effected more or less by the touch of a button. In the early years, machine translation yielded usable text only in the case of very straightforward, repetitive, factual source texts, in a handful of standard languages. Increasingly, though, machine translation is benefiting from the advances of artificial intelligence and machine learning, and the range of supported languages is increasing all the time – though the Hebrew and Aramaic involved in the Bible project would certainly still overtax current capabilities. While the challenges in machine interpreting are more complex, similar advances are coming in this field, too. So how much scope for human involvement is there likely to be in the future? Both the early modern Bible project and current provision of machine translation services shed light on this question.

Production of language is always a creative process, even if the elements are conventional. Like a political speech, a translation will only communicate successfully if it speaks effectively to its audience. This means it needs to be appropriate in content and style, and translation will therefore tend to involve some degree of adaptation. For example, translating a Spanish text into English for a maximally international audience will involve aiming for a style that is culturally and stylistically as neutral as possible, avoiding both specifically American and specifically British expressions, while choosing American spelling since this will be more appropriate for global reach. Meanwhile 'localizing' the same text for a British audience will require British spelling and favour use of British expressions.

Such choices have faced Bible translators through the ages. This can be traced in translations of the Hebrew phrase 'to cover his feet' in the following verse, rendered thus in the King James Bible: 'And [Saul] came to the sheepcotes by the way, where was a cave; and Saul went in to cover his feet' (I Sam. 24:3). The translation conveys the literal meaning of the expression but leaves modern English-speaking readers puzzled as to what is meant, whereas the Jewish audience would have understood it as a euphemism for 'to evacuate his bowels'. Seventeenth-century translators are likely to have understood that meaning, but like the creators of the Hebrew text, they avoided reference to a taboo bodily function – even though in English this obscures the actual meaning. In fact in the previous century, the Bible translator Martin Luther evidently considered a transparent rendering for his German version: his manuscript has *scheißen* (to shit), but he evidently shied away from this in print, instead giving the literal translation of the words like King James's translators. Bible translators in modern times have continued to grapple with this issue. *The Living Bible* has a policy of creating a text that communicates clearly with the modern reader and has gone for localization. While the British edition gives 'to relieve himself', the North American edition has 'Saul went into a cave to go to the bathroom'.[4] Which of these options is most appropriate for a particular audience requires the individual judgement of a human translator, with new translations becoming necessary as audiences, languages and cultural norms change.

Taking account of the purpose of a translation is as important as attending to its audience, and the two aspects are indeed interdependent. When King James VI (of Scotland) and I (of England and Ireland) convened his team of translators after acceding to the English throne in 1603, his purpose was not to produce a translation of the Bible because none existed. It was to put his stamp on a version that would provide the textual foundation for his vision of the Church of England – a purpose not unlike that of Ptolemy V establishing his religious cult with the multilingual decree recorded on the Rosetta Stone. Accordingly, King James's team of translators produced their version of the Bible in a combination of editing and translating on the basis of his instructions.

This is in principle not significantly different to the work of a modern translator using machine translation. While the machine will produce an initial translated output, the translator will scrutinize, edit, modify, localize and customize it in order to ensure that the finished translation fulfils the purpose intended by the commissioning party. In the case of a complex legal document, for example, it is likely to remain more efficient to produce the translation directly, without the aid of machine translation. Meanwhile an advertising text might require a rewrite. And in the case of a literary work commissioned by a publisher, the involvement of unique creativity will often be a key criterion for the purpose, suitability and success of the translation.

Translation and interpreting are a key part of what is encompassed by 'communications' or 'comms'. Communications fulfil a key role for any organization as the interface between its work and the audiences for which that work is intended. Globalization has immeasurably increased the international dimension of what organizations do, and also the cultural and linguistic complexity of audiences within a country. Human judgement is essential for any cross-linguistic, cross-cultural task that requires deep understanding of the contexts involved, and sensitivity towards diversity. When studying languages, translation is invaluable in training precision of language use, and appreciation of subtle nuances of meaning in the two languages involved. Moreover, it heightens awareness of stylistic quality and sensitivity towards cultural difference.

4

Training Cultural
Intelligence

Cultural diversity is a feature of the human condition, and with globalization it is becoming an increasingly prominent feature of life in schools, workforces and society more generally. The study of modern languages is vitally important in this context because it develops awareness of the crucial role languages play in shaping and expressing distinctive identities. How we experience cultural diversity individually, and to what extent we are aware of it, varies enormously and depends in part on the society we live in. Some people grow up in culturally homogeneous homes and communities, and encounter other cultures primarily if they travel. For others, engaging with different cultures is part of everyday life. Diversity of languages is part of the fabric of multiculturalism, though societies vary in the extent to which they recognize linguistic diversity as significant and respect it as an intrinsic part of cultural life. In the United Kingdom, France and Germany, citizens are expected to speak, or learn, a single dominant or official language: English, French and German respectively. Meanwhile South Africa, for example, recognizes eleven official languages, with calls for the addition of South African Sign Language – though there may of course be significant discrepancies between stated policy and reality on the ground, and many other languages spoken in the country do not have recognized status. Divergences of cultural context and experience give us differing awareness of cultural variation and its effects, differing views concerning the value it has for society as a whole, and differing expertise in handling such diversity in our daily interactions with people.

Studying modern languages immeasurably enhances appreciation of the many ways in which multiculturalism connects with multilingualism, and how important languages are for cultural identity. Increasingly, all areas of people's lives are touched by multiculturalism, and globalization has raised the public profile of cultural diversity. Societies which in the twentieth century tended to see themselves as monocultural are gradually accommodating themselves to being more multicultural;

schools are adjusting to teaching a large proportion of children whose first language, spoken at home, differs from the language established in that society as standard, or official; and businesses are increasingly recognizing not only the challenges of having multicultural workforces, but also the significant business opportunities that arise from their internal diversity. In anglophone countries, however, there tends to be insufficient understanding of the need to factor languages into that cultural diversity.

The Role of Languages in Cultural Intelligence

It is not, then, a matter of chance that the beginning of the twenty-first century saw the emergence of the concept of 'cultural intelligence'.[1] While it was initially developed with reference especially to business, it was soon extended to other types of organization and has now become established in more general use. The purpose here is not to address or adopt it as a technical concept or to subscribe to a particular theory of what cultural intelligence is, or how it might be assessed, let alone measured and quantified. Rather, the purpose here is to highlight the vital importance modern languages has in this field, and to explore what it can contribute to our understanding of cultural intelligence, taken as a mainstream concept that is fundamental to intercultural relations, from families and local communities, schools and workplaces through to organizations that shape our social lives. A related term that has come to the fore in recent years is 'cultural literacy', and we might also refer more generally to 'cultural competence'. What matters is to ensure that the interaction between languages and cultures is kept in view as a key element in the debate.

Modern languages as a discipline is centrally concerned with developing cultural intelligence. Language learning involves systematic training in cultural differences, for example the use of polite and familiar forms of address. And the study of literature or film develops heightened sensitivity towards the diversity of cultural values and beliefs that shape human actions. Students encounter scenarios where cultural norms and expectations may differ markedly from those prevailing in their own context. An example is the role of honour in 'wife-murder' plays of the seventeenth-century Spanish playwright Pedro Calderón de la Barca. Without an awareness of the central significance *honor* had in that society, and what precisely was associated with it in terms of social norms, we can't interpret the plays appropriately. By immersing ourselves in that very different world, we become more sensitive to cultural differences and the importance of attending to their implications for human relationships. Studying languages in interaction with their cultural contexts is ideally suited to enhancing understanding of a dimension that anglocentric theories of cultural intelligence tend to ignore: the crucial significance of linguistic diversity for the formation and expression of cultural identity, and all forms of cross-cultural exchange.

It is in the nature of cultural and linguistic diversity that we can only ever glimpse a tiny part of the whole range. This might suggest that in training cultural intelligence, the focus should be on studying the theory of cultural and linguistic diversity. However, while this can provide a useful framework for policymaking and study, it needs to be complemented by first-hand experience of diverse cultural and linguistic practice. Turning to an analogy: a chef wanting to extend their cultural repertoire will not just read recipe books – they will taste real dishes, cooked by people with the relevant cultural heritage.

Immersion in another cultural and linguistic universe makes us keenly aware of differences and similarities by comparison with the world we are familiar with, and it opens our mind to intriguing contrasts, fruitful tensions and exciting discoveries. Such experience is not quantifiable. Whether we study one language and culture in depth, in addition to what we are familiar with, or whether we range more widely and comparatively, and whether we study languages and cultures that differ significantly from each other or ones that are closely related – each perspective will enrich our understanding of how culture and language interact, making us more culturally aware and more sensitive to the significance and impacts of difference.

Does Language Influence How We Think?

The process of learning a language and becoming familiar with contexts in which it is used takes us deep into the question of 'linguistic relativity' or 'linguistic relativism', a highly contentious issue in philosophy and linguistics that is often discussed under the heading of the 'Sapir–Whorf hypothesis' (referring to the work of the anthropological linguists Edward Sapir and Benjamin Whorf). Whorf made the following claim: 'We dissect nature along lines laid down by our native languages. . . . The world is presented in a kaleidoscopic flux of impressions which has to be organized by our minds – and this means largely by the linguistic systems in our minds.'[2] Whorf's professional standing, research methods and findings have been extensively called into question, discredited and ridiculed in linguistics,[3] and certainly the use of 'largely' in the above statement is open to question. There is, however, evidence that thought and language influence each other.

An area where the interplay between thought and language has been explored in depth is metaphorical conceptualizations of time, which differ significantly across cultures. Evidence of interdependence between language and thought has been established in a number of studies. For example, an experiment in the field of psychology found that Mandarin speakers were more inclined to use vertical metaphors for time than English speakers, and that they correspondingly showed a greater tendency to conceptualize time in vertical terms. In another study, temporal ordering of events was found to reflect the directionality of reading prevailing in the dominant writing system: while test subjects speaking a language using a script such as Latin, which is read from left to right, correspondingly ordered events from left to right, the opposite was the case with test subjects using a script that is read from right to left, such as Arabic or Hebrew.[4]

Whole fields of knowledge can be shaped by concepts and the words that express them. For example, the German word *Wissenschaft* with its plural *Wissenschaften* and associated adjective *wissenschaftlich* seamlessly encompasses the whole range of academic disciplines, ranging from the *Geisteswissenschaften* (arts and humanities) and *Sozialwissenschaften* (social sciences) through to the *Naturwissenschaften* (natural sciences). The concept creates a space in which all forms of knowledge and research are in principle equal. Being used to thinking in terms of a single overarching concept, and having a term for it, Germans seeking to translate the words *Wissenschaft* and *wissenschaftlich* into English will be inclined to look for a single word that similarly encompasses all disciplines – with the solution tending to be 'science(s)' and 'scientific'. This in turn holds the danger of privileging one type of knowledge and research while others are automatically rendered invisible.

The fact that knowledge, research and science are conceptualized in subtly different ways even just between German and English highlights the need for different languages to be part of the academic conversation. That conversation must involve researchers across the world, as argued with reference to pandemics in an article in the

Smithsonian Magazine entitled 'English is the language of science. That isn't always a good thing', with an explanation provided in the subtitle: 'How a bias toward English-language science can result in preventable crises, duplicated efforts and lost knowledge'.[5] Beyond that consideration, restricting sciences to one language reduces our options for thinking outside familiar mental boxes and diminishes our potential for finding new solutions to global challenges.

This issue has critical implications for knowledge about the natural environment and the methods that are informed by the ways in which we structure that knowledge. A people that has lived for centuries in a particular place, knowing and naming local plants, insects, birds and other animals, will have a more multifaceted and holistic understanding of that environment than city-dwellers in other countries. The indigenous population will know, and have special names for, animal habitats, medicinal properties of plants, effects of weather and interactions between different parts of the biological system, with their own ways of classifying natural knowledge and conceptualizing the relationship between humans, animals, plants, land and sea. Respecting the cultural difference of which language forms a crucial part is vital in preserving diversity for the benefit of all. This objective was enshrined in the following declaration by the United Nations Environment Programme (UNEP) in 2007: 'Biodiversity also incorporates human cultural diversity, which can be affected by the same drivers as biodiversity, and which has impacts on the diversity of genes, other species, and ecosystems.'[6] This policy statement led to recognition of the new concept of 'biocultural diversity'. Cultural intelligence needs to include an appreciation of how vitally languages contribute both to culture and to knowledge.

Cultural Intelligence in Practice

While 'cultural intelligence' was only established as a formal concept in the early twenty-first century, we may safely assume that as a basic capability, it comes naturally to human beings as social creatures with a long history of migration and cultural exchange. Giving it a name lends it value, and establishing criteria for measuring it makes it into a commodity. There is no need to pursue or indeed accept the measurability and commodification of the concept. It is, however, worth noting that cultural intelligence is a supremely valuable transferable skill in a world that is increasingly characterized by movement,

71

interaction and tension between cultural groups at all levels of global and local society. Moreover, it is a transferable skill that connects directly with the value of language skills, and it helps to explain why studying modern languages matters.

In order to elucidate the value of cultural intelligence, and the relevance of languages in that context, it is useful to consider a scenario that might play out in any small or large modern workplace in a country that perceives itself as monolingual. The social and political context is relevant, since it sets important cultural parameters, with organizations and individuals taking their cue from political role models and policies. For example, in England, the United Kingdom's 2016 referendum vote to leave the European Union brought a surge of nationalism that was accompanied by the increasingly vocal and sometimes violently articulated view that people ought to speak English in public.

This development prompted street magazine *The Big Issue* to come out against 'language vigilantes' in an article entitled 'Using more than one language matters now more than ever'.[7] The article highlighted two key themes in a range of episodes reported in the press: 'ownership' and 'suspicion'. In practice, this means that individuals who perceive themselves as part of the dominant and empowered group project themselves as 'owning' the relevant public space. Meanwhile, perception of difference becomes suspicion that the 'other' poses a threat, fostering a wish to exclude what is regarded as alien.

A sense of linguistic ownership of an environment or organization, and suspicion of linguistic difference, are most likely among people who have not themselves been given the opportunity to identify with speaking a language other than the one that is dominant in their society. The study of modern languages gives individuals the opportunity to experience language difference first-hand, and overcome distrust of people who speak another language as being 'foreign' and 'not one of us'. Transferred to work in an organization, such experience offers a strong foundation for generating solutions that build bridges between groups and foster a culture of inclusivity. Developing cultural intelligence consistently in the course of studying the complex interplay between language and culture can open up significant career opportunities, for global workplaces of all kinds need people with cultural intelligence in every part of the organization. Moreover, there is the added bonus that cultural intelligence is invaluable also in private life.

Recognizing Limits

The world of translation is full of amusing anecdotes showing how badly companies get things wrong when they fail to appreciate potential linguistic and cultural pitfalls in exporting their products. The United Kingdom alone is estimated to lose around 3.5% of annual national income because of 'language ignorance',[8] with localization mistakes being one factor among many that stand in the way of export success. They range from mistranslations of advertising slogans through contraventions of cultural taboos to unintended sexual meanings of brand and product names and advertising slogans. One translation agency cites examples including the following: 'Vicks Cough Drops had to change their name to Wicks in the German market because the pronunciation was too close to a vulgar term for sexual penetration; Puffs brand tissues didn't play well in the German market either, where "puff" is a colloquialism for a brothel.'[9]

Choosing the right level of formality can also be tricky in languages that have a familiar and a polite form of 'you', such as *tu* and *vous* in French, *tú* and *usted* in Spanish or *du* and *Sie* in German. Which form is appropriate varies not only between languages but also within them. The familiar form is used much more widely in Spanish than in French or German, but in Spanish-speaking countries in Latin America, it is used less widely than in Spain, with regional differences and variation by class also playing a part. Especially coming from a language such as English, which makes no distinction, and an anglophone culture where first names are used very readily, local expertise is necessary to ensure that communication is appropriate to the audience.

Sensitivity to linguistic identity in interaction with cultural identity can play a decisive part in export marketing, as the Japanese company Nintendo found in 2016 when it decided to move away from its previous practice of localizing the names of its Pokémon characters for different parts of the Chinese-speaking world. The name of the popular character Pikachu had previously been translated into Mandarin (spoken in mainland China) as 'Pi-Ka-Qiu', and into Cantonese (spoken in Hong Kong) as 'Bei-Ka-Ciu'. Nintendo now abandoned the Cantonese version in favour of the Mandarin version, written 皮卡丘. In Cantonese, this would be pronounced Pei-ka-yau, and people in Hong Kong complained that it sounded quite different from Pikachu. The controversy went viral when Hong Kong protesters took to the streets and demonstrated outside the Japanese embassy. The *Japan Times* reported the following comment from one of the protestors: 'The Chinese names resonating with Cantonese pronunciation have been in use for some 20 years and fully reflected Hong Kong's culture. Nintendo has now become an accomplice to the political agenda of "promote Putonghua [Mandarin], eradicate Cantonese".'[10] According to a BBC report on the protest, 'The dispute taps into growing local fears that Cantonese – along with local culture and tradition – is being supplanted by Mandarin.'[11]

In commercial terms, Nintendo's change in marketing strategy posed the risk of alienating an important target group, though this may have been compensated by the efficiency gains of simplification. The repercussions became political because the change took place in the context of political tensions between mainland China and Hong Kong, and a far-reaching Chinese language policy seen by the protesters as a threat to Hong Kong's political and cultural independence. The complex relationship between the spoken language and the writing system attained critical importance because it is deeply connected with, and legitimizes, the diversity among varieties of Chinese while embodying the long tradition of classical Chinese culture (see Figure 4). The Chinese government is, by contrast, engaged in a drive to establish standardization and

Figure 4. Whereas the People's Republic of China has imposed simplified characters as the standard script for Chinese languages, speakers of Cantonese in Hong Kong value the traditional Chinese script, used by this street artist.

© Anthony Kwan/Stringer/Getty

broadly based literacy by privileging Mandarin, the Beijing-based spoken variety, and simplifying the system of characters.[12] The Hong Kong protesters' concern about the linguistic identity of a fictional character was founded on an acute awareness of the power language can exert as a tool of cultural and political control.

As is evident from this example, a key part of

cultural intelligence is understanding what role language plays in a given situation. The authors of the book that first established the concept of cultural intelligence (CQ) use an anecdote about cross-linguistic communication to highlight the need for cultural intelligence to encompass effective adaptation to cultural context:

> The first author (a non-native Chinese speaker who has attempted to learn Chinese) had a well-intentioned Western colleague who had prepared a careful speech in Chinese to show his Chinese colleagues his appreciation for their hospital-ity. After listening to the American's speech one of the Chinese professors commented (well out of hearing range of the American so as to avoid offending him), 'I really appreciated his trying to give his speech, but I had absolutely no idea what he was saying.' The American seemed unable to produce the appropriate tones during his speech even though he had the correct 'words'. Our point is that without effective execution, a person's CQ is not realized. CQ requires effective adaptation to cultural circumstance – not merely one's thoughts, intentions, or wishes.[13]

Like communication skills more generally, foreign-language skills are most useful and effective if their use is embedded in a broad understanding of cultural context. Part of that is being able to assess what linguistic mode of expression will best serve the specific purpose. A connection is evident here with the classical tradition of rhetoric, in which it is axiomatic that the speaker should attend to the effect of their speech on the audience. What additionally comes into play is an understanding of one's own limits, and when to call in specialist expertise. Developing good judgement of this kind is beneficial in any field, and it forms an essen tial foundation on which to build fruitful cultural exchange.

5

Developing the Imagination

Studying a language engages every part of the self and sense of self. It stretches our powers of analysis and memory, it makes us talk differently, and it takes us along new pathways of thought. It is always enriching, and it can also be fun and exciting – never more so than when we immerse ourselves imaginatively in a new world through the creative arts. This might be music or computer games, opera or theatre, fiction or film. Our powers of imagination are activated when we read stories or poems, watch plays or movies, listen to music or imagine that we are part of a scenario as a participant or as the person pulling the strings that make things happen. Creative writing can liberate our powers of language, permitting a use of forms that may be 'wrong' in the classroom but effective in an experimental poem that could be bilingual or multilingual.

Our imagination enables us to create a whole world in our mind – it is the stuff that dreams are made of, and also a power we need in our daily lives to think creatively and imagine a reality that is different to what we are used to.

Reading great 'canonical' literature has traditionally played an important part in modern languages courses, since studying works that are recognized by speakers of the language as forming pinnacles of their written culture offers first-hand experience of the language at its most complex and creative. Grappling with the challenge of reading – in the original language – Dante's *Divine Comedy*, Tolstoy's *War and Peace* or a French medieval epic, or engaging closely with Spanish Golden Age drama or Japanese Noh Theatre, are cultural equivalents of climbing peaks in the Himalayas. The process of understanding the work develops an appreciation of the values enshrined in the artefacts, and gives multifaceted insights into ways of life that are very different to our own.

The cultural foothills offer other rewards, as do the mines underground in which lie works that have been forgotten, even though they may have been very popular in their era. Feminist research has brought authors to the fore who were denied the recognition they deserved by lacking publishing opportunities or by being consigned to the margins of male-centred literary history. And movements such as LGBTQ+ or #BlackLivesMatter are continually prompting reappraisals of literary voices, and reconfigurations of syllabuses. Our understanding of what is valuable in culture, and art, changes over time, and we may find that different types of work engage us imaginatively in different ways.

Straight to the Heart

All the arts involve language in some way – as a medium, in titles, in the associated discourse that contributes to their meaning and dissemination – and different cultures develop fascinatingly diverse interpretations of art forms, which are continually on the move. Western popular music is an example. Since the advent of pop groups and rock bands such as the Beatles and the Rolling Stones, it has tended to be markedly anglocentric, especially from the perspective of English-speaking countries, and this has indeed been a factor promoting 'global English' across the world. However, some artists succeed in appealing to international audiences in languages other than English, often drawing creatively on their national traditions and at times indeed on national stereotypes: Kraftwerk and Rammstein, for example, exude 'hard' Germanic qualities even with their choice of name while then also drawing on the German Romantic tradition.

Adopting a vantage point in another culture will bring a wide variety of voices to the fore that can offer intriguing pathways into seams of tradition that may lead to unexpected places. Music in itself stimulates the emotions and the imagination, an effect that is enhanced when it interacts with language in poetic form. Moreover, with the advent of electronic media, a visual dimension will often enrich the experience further, creating a kind of *Gesamtkunstwerk* – a term coined by Richard Wagner to designate an artistic synthesis exemplified by the 'all-encompassing artistic works' he strove for with his operas. Music videos created by contemporary artists to enhance their albums are a far cry from Wagner, but they rely on a similar synthesis of art forms for their appeal to the emotions through the ear, eye and imagination.

The Belgian singer-songwriter Stromae (Paul Van Haver) plays with language in his stage name, created from an inversion of the syllables in the Italian word *maestro*. While alluding to the 'high' musical tradition, he has transformed the word into *verlan*, a form of popular backslang that puts the syllables 'back to front' (*à l'envers* → *vers+l'en*), as he explains in a performative bilingual TED talk.[1] Stromae sets his work in the tradition of Belgian singer-songwriter Jacques Brel and draws on a wide range of popular traditions, including percussion and dance elements reminiscent of his own partially African roots. His lyrics are entertainingly light-touch, often with archetypically French titles such as 'Formidable' ('Wonderful', 'Fantastic') or 'Moules Frites' ('Mussels and Fries'), though also with more thought-provoking themes. The song 'Papaoutai' (2013)[2] – a free spelling of 'Papa, où t'es?' or 'Dad, where are you?' – suggests an allusion to the loss of his father in the Rwandan genocide against the Tutsi in 1994, a tragedy in Belgian postcolonial history. The song gains its multi-layered meaning as much from the interplay between fathers and sons in the video as from the lyrics, with dance moves and clothing appealing to the imagination with multimodal effects. Stromae's vocal delivery is distinctively laid-back and attuned to dance rhythms while also being reminiscent of the French *chanson* tradition in foregrounding the sensuous sound of the French language.

The Catalan singer-songwriter Rosalía (Rosalía Vila Tobella) draws on the tradition of flamenco, on the basis of a rigorous musical training in the art form. Singing primarily in Spanish, she fuses flamenco with a multitude of other musical styles, and incorporates a wide range of dance sequences in her music videos. With her album *El Mal Querer* (The Bad Loving, 2018), she constructs a narrative flamenco tradition reaching back to the Middle Ages, in eleven 'chapters' that allude to the romance *Flamenca*, a tale in which the eponymous Flemish (*flamenca*) heroine is kept locked up by her jealous husband, though she conducts an illicit relationship with a lover disguised as a priest.[3] The medieval narrative is in Occitan, a Romance language closely related to Catalan and spoken in Catalonia and the south of France, while flamenco originated later, in Andalusia in southern Spain. The allusion to the literary source grounds the album in a story of toxic love. The second song, 'Que no salga la luna' (Don't let the moon rise),[4] most overtly exhibits features of flamenco and recalls an iconic Spanish tragedy: Federico García Lorca's play *Bodas de sangre* (Blood Wedding, 1933). The video of the first song, 'Malamente',[5] includes visual allusions to bullfighting in male dance moves, picking up on the most famous Spanish stereotype of all.

Rosalía is a consummate artist who operates at a complex interface between local, creatively interpreted cultural tradition and a global arts scene that reaches its audience primarily via multimodal electronic media. In *El Mal Querer* she constructs a heritage for flamenco that connects her performance, and her (Catalan rather than Andalusian) cultural community, to a rich and colourful performative tradition. She thereby draws on an age-old practice of discovering and/or creating cultural and linguistic roots as a means of enhancing the value of cultural and linguistic practices in the present. (Another example is the tradition of Welsh *eisteddfods* discussed in Chapter 1, which are only somewhat tenuously established in documented history.) By fashioning a coherent, strikingly Hispanic narrative, Rosalía engages her audience's imagination in valuing present practices as part of an enduring tradition in which the individual is building their legacy. Rosalía's lyrics have attracted extensive interpretation from fans on social media channels, and also elucidation intended to inspire fans to learn Spanish so they may appreciate her emotive songs more fully.[6] As with Stromae's performances, Rosalía's songs draw their energy above all from her expressive use of voice.

Studying an artistic work takes us into a cultural tradition from a particular entry point, giving insights into a moment in time while also opening up a particular route into the past. Language is an intrinsic part of the contemporary context and its history, and understanding the language enables us to connect immediately with the imaginative world that is opened up by the work. Sound plays an important role because it affects us viscerally. Our innate sensitivity to subtle differences between languages, already developed at birth (see Chapter 1), demonstrates how extraordinarily attuned we are to the effects of vocal articulation. Music helps even a foreign language to reach our heart. Engaging with what the words mean, and appreciating the cultural heritage from which they gain their resonance, makes for an even richer imaginative experience.

Creative Subversions

Film has an important place in studying modern languages because it can give us a realistic insight into a cultural world that is associated with the language that is being learned – a world in which the language is spoken naturally and used for normal everyday purposes. Yet film also offers a space for probing social norms and pushing the boundaries of social convention, with experimental techniques serving to question tradition also in artistic terms. The provocative potential of film is exemplified in the work of Spanish filmmaker Pedro Almodóvar, who came to the fore at a time when Spain was experiencing the seismic change occasioned by the death of the 'Generalissimo', fascist dictator Francisco Franco. He had ruled the country from 1939 to 1975, and the sense of liberation was immense, especially among the younger generation. Cutting across categories of 'high' versus 'low' art, Almodóvar's films are entertaining and thought-provoking, touching and hard-hitting, aesthetically sumptuous and at times repulsive, each one different.

While gender roles in some rural parts of Spain still follow highly traditional patterns, Almodóvar's films are inspired by social life in the country's capital, Madrid. They transgress every kind of sexual boundary, featuring characters who are straight, gay, transgender or transvestite, who engage variously in consensual sex and masturbation, incest and prostitution, bondage and rape. Yet what drives Almodóvar is not the objective to shock as such. Rather, he seeks to open up a space where his characters have the liberty to express their personal identities as morally autonomous individuals.[7]

His films comment on, and play with, traditional family models and gender stereotypes, but above all subvert them. The early black comedy *¿Qué he hecho yo para merecer esto?* (What Have I Done to

Deserve This?, 1984) centres on the dysfunctional relationship between a downtrodden housewife and her husband in the family's overcrowded apartment, and it turns into a husband-murder plot when he dies after she hits him over the head with a leg of ham. *Matador* (1986) takes the subversion of gender stereotypes celebrated in bullfighting to a melodramatic extreme, giving murderous agency to María, a lawyer, who stabs her lover and fellow murderer Diego, a former bullfighter, before shooting herself as they make love. *Todo sobre mi madre* (All About My Mother, 1999) opens up a world of non-traditional gender relations, focusing on single mother Manuela's loss of her son in a car accident and search for the son's transgender other parent Lola. *Volver* (Come Back, 2006) depicts a family consisting entirely of women – sisters Raimunda and Sole, their dementia-stricken aunt Paula, the (assumed) ghost of their mother Irene and Raimunda's daughter Paula. Almodóvar works with strong female actors, and women are at the centre of his films, empowered even in the most adverse circumstances.

Almodóvar's craft as a filmmaker encompasses careful selection of music and meticulous attention to language. In accordance with the nationally recognized standard, he favours Castilian, the form of Spanish spoken in Madrid. In an interview for a French film magazine, he comments on his avoidance of mixed accents and exclusion of Catalan, Canarian Spanish and Latin American Spanish from his films because he finds them 'disturbing'. Dubbing comes in for even stronger opprobrium as a 'legacy of Nazism'. The rationale for both judgements is evident in his description (in French) of his work with the actors: 'C'est vrai que je travaille beaucoup la musicalité des dialogues. J'oblige les acteurs à un entraînement où je leur explique très en détails comment je veux qu'ils prononcent les mots' (It's true that I work a lot on the musicality of the dialogues. I require the actors to engage in training where I explain to them in great detail how I want them to pronounce the words).[8] The accent, rhythm and pace of the dialogue are intrinsic to the artistic identity and quality of the films.

Almodóvar's rejection of dubbing raises far-reaching questions concerning the global dissemination of art that involves the spoken language. In the medium of film, translation in the form of subtitling must always leave a lot out, but it allows us to hear the original voices. Translation in the form of dubbing converts the words into another language but it inevitably obliterates the carefully chosen and trained individual voices that are central to the

Developing the Imagination

artistic effect of the work. Almodóvar's fascinating characters, surprising plots, rich use of colour and bold cinematic effects make his films rewarding in any language. But familiarity with Spanish allows the viewer to fully appreciate the musicality of dialogue and nuances of meaning that contribute to the richness of these works of art.

Stimulating the Imagination

Studying fiction can take us back into the past and allow us to enter the mind of someone who lived in an earlier era. It will often take us on a journey to a different part of the world. It may enable us to time-travel and inhabit a world created with the techniques of science fiction. Across many different eras and traditions, people have created stories that allow us to escape from the here and now, discover worlds different from our own, and look at familiar things in new ways. How do narratives achieve this? Two iconic twentieth-century works of fiction will serve to give glimpses of how narrative processes can stimulate our imagination and inspire us to explore meaning: *Die Verwandlung* (The Metamorphosis, 1915) by Franz Kafka and *La Peste* (The Plague, 1947) by Albert Camus.

91

Kafka grew up in Prague – then part of the Austro-Hungarian Empire and now capital of the Czech Republic – as a member of the German-speaking community there. Camus was a French citizen who grew up in Algeria, at that time a French colony. Both works are 'timeless' in that they communicate immediately with the reader without depending on knowledge of the language in which they were written, or knowledge of their origin. However, in both cases, reading them in the original enriches our understanding.

Kafka's short story opens with the protagonist Gregor's experience of waking up one morning:

Als Gregor Samsa eines Morgens aus unruhigen Träumen erwachte, fand er sich in seinem Bett zu einem ungeheueren Ungeziefer verwandelt. Er lag auf seinem panzerartig harten Rücken und sah, wenn er den Kopf ein wenig hob, seinen gewölbten, braunen, von bogenförmigen Versteifungen geteilten Bauch [. . .]. 'Was ist mit mir geschehen?' dachte er. Es war kein Traum.

(When Gregor Samsa awoke one morning from troubled dreams, he found himself changed into a monstrous cockroach in his bed. He lay on his tough, armoured back, and, raising his head a little, managed to see – sectioned off by little crescent-shaped ridges into segments – the expanse of his arched, brown belly [. . .]. 'What's the matter with me?' he thought. It was no dream.)[9]

Kafka draws on the narrative technique of 'free indirect discourse', widely used in realist fiction, to create a remarkable fusion of the real and the surreal. He achieves this by combining devices which suggest external objectivity with devices that take us inside the mind of Gregor, a travelling salesman, who finds himself unable to go to work as normal. A third-person 'outside' perspective ('Gregor Samsa [. . .] he') suggests that an objective narrator of a past event is recounting facts. This is confirmed by the realistic focus on Gregor's physical form and, subsequently, comments on the movement of his limbs and the dimensions of his physical room. These concrete details lend truth value to the statement of an unequivocal conclusion: 'Es war kein Traum' ('It was no dream'), stated by the narrator rather than quoted from Gregor's thoughts like the question that precedes the statement.

Yet the detail is conveyed from inside Gregor's mind as he takes in what his eyes see ('He [. . .] managed to see') and then asks himself, 'Was ist mit mir geschehen?' (rendered in this translation by Michael Hofmann as 'What's the matter with me?' – or, more accurately, 'What has happened to me?').

Developing the Imagination

Owing to the precision of Gregor's perceptions and his surprise when perceiving his transformed body, the reader unquestioningly assumes that this creature is mentally a human being. His systematic observations concerning his body, and his measured question in response to the transformation, convey that this individual is not inclined to exaggerate, or to overreact to the unexpected. In fact, he is quite extraordinarily rational.

Every detail of this beginning removes the possibility of interpreting the transformation as 'merely a dream' or as 'just in the mind'. It pushes us to delve further into the meaning of the narrative and look for clues that might explain what kind of 'Verwandlung' is at stake. The central event to which Gregor is responding is defined in the statement that he 'found himself changed' – 'fand er sich [. . .] verwandelt'. The German verb connects explicitly with the title of the story while the past participle form establishes that the event has already happened before the start of the story. No agent is given and no evident explanation is offered at any point. One clue may be Gregor's potentially excessive rationality. Another is the designation 'ungeheueres Ungeziefer' with its repeated negative prefix *un-*. Translators have opted for many possible near-equivalents of the German noun, for example 'insect', 'beetle', 'bug' or, here, 'cockroach'. The German in fact leaves the species undefined, though *un-* conveys that the creature is shunned 'vermin'. And while the adjective *ungeheuer* means 'enormous' or 'gigantic', the equivalent noun *das Ungeheuer* means 'monster', as is conveyed here in the translation 'monstrous'. In the course of the story, Kafka opens up ever new dimensions to enrich the possible interpretations, without allowing us to 'arrive' at a definitive meaning. By vividly fusing the real with the surreal, he creates an effect that has become known as 'Kafkaesque'.

Vermin also play an important part in Camus' *La Peste* – cast here in realistic form as grotesquely perishing rats transmitting deadly disease (Figure 5). Whereas *Die Verwandlung*, written in early twentieth-century Prague and set in a modern flat, is otherwise geographically featureless, *La Peste* is geographically and historically specific. The narrator begins by specifying time and place, and defines his genre as one that recounts historical facts: 'Les curieux événements qui font le sujet de cette chronique se sont produits en 194., à Oran' (The unusual events described in this chronicle occurred in 194–, at Oran).[10] The city is situated explicitly on the Algerian coast, with the date potentially suggesting Oran's period under collaborationist Vichy rule in

Figure 5. Albert Camus, *La Peste* (Le Livre de Poche 132) (Paris: Gallimard, 1947), cover of the first paperback edition. The cover depicts the French colonial city of Oran, on the Algerian coast, being invaded by rats bringing the bubonic plague.

Librairie Gallimard/Le Livre de Poche

1940–2. The city's French authorities are answerable to the administration in France as they deal with Bernard Rieux, the doctor who is both the narrator and the main character. The novel depicts the world of French colonialism and is at the same time a product of it, as becomes evident especially when it is read in the original: although it is set in North Africa, there is no mention of non-French communities and no occasion to depart from French even in the characters' names. This selectively presented, but emphatically real, 'completely modern'[11] colonial city suddenly succumbs to the ravaging spread of the bubonic plague – associated by the citizens of Oran and by the reader with the stuff of medieval and early modern history: the Black Death.

The reader follows Rieux as he goes about his daily work and grows aware of the dying rats and unusual symptoms among the people of Oran. A key theme in the first part of the novel is the challenge this outbreak of an assumedly obsolete disease poses for the imagination. Rieux, as a doctor who has reflected on suffering, credits himself with 'un peu plus d'imagination' (somewhat more imagination) than the average person, but even he finds it difficult to make the connection between what he has read about historical plague outbreaks and what he is witnessing with his own eyes.[12] Convinced by the scientific evidence and statistical figures, he faces an uphill struggle persuading the local government authorities to procure the necessary equipment and implement appropriate isolation and burial measures. Commenting to a friend that the measures are hardly adequate for 'un rhume de cerveau' (a common cold), he concludes: 'Ce qui leur manque, c'est l'imagination' (What they're short of is imagination).[13] He also notes that the response of the public is slower than might have been expected: 'L'annonce que la troisième semaine de peste avait compté trois cent deux morts ne parlait pas à l'imagination' (The bare statement that three hundred and two deaths had taken place in the third week of plague failed to strike their imagination).[14] The reader is taken into a world of individual and collective suffering, and prompted by the narrator's experiences to reflect on its implications for how we think.

Camus prefaces the novel with a quotation (in French translation) from Daniel Defoe's *Robinson Crusoe*: "'tis as reasonable to represent one kind of Imprisonment by another, as it is to represent any Thing that really exists, by that which exists not.'[15] The English translation by Stuart Gilbert inexplicably omits the quotation. Yet it is important, for it provides a perspective beyond the community depicted in the narrative and invites reading the novel on different levels.[16] In the post-war decades, the analogy with the era of fascism seemed most salient, given the setting in a city ruled by the Vichy government, the date of 194- and motifs including the invasion by vermin, closure of the city, restrictive legislation, themes of exile and revolt and eventual liberation. Each of these elements can be invested with symbolic value, which gives the narrator's final comment the force of a political warning when he foregrounds his awareness that the plague bacillus never dies and may send forth its rats again, 'pour le malheur et l'enseignement des hommes' (for the bane and the enlightening of men).[17]

Events can change our interpretations, as is evident with this novel, which saw an immediate rise in popularity during 2020 in the context of the Covid-19 pandemic. Readers now were struck by the novel's realism as they followed the epidemic's impact on every part of society and every habit of lifestyle. The failures of the imagination exhibited by the authorities and the general public in Oran connected directly with the lived experience of actual responses to a very real modern epidemic.

Camus' novel *La Peste* demonstrates that imagination is not just a cultural luxury. The uncanny parallels between the response to a fictional epidemic in 1940s Oran and the global response to a real pandemic in 2020 suggest that it is a vital resource for human survival. Interpreting literature from another culture, in another language, immerses us in scenarios we have never experienced first-hand, training our imagination to conceive the impossible.

6

Negotiating Globalization

Modern languages as a discipline is ideally placed to engage with globalization and the tensions it engenders. Globalization is affecting every part of the world, in a multitude of ways that are creating continually changing constellations of language distribution and language use. One might say that it has always been at work in human history, with populations migrating and eventually inhabiting all continents. Yet the concept and term 'globalization' only arose in the twentieth century – the *Oxford English Dictionary* notes its first recorded uses in French in 1904 and English in 1930. The new concept captures a new dynamic: the 'action, process, or fact of making global', as the *OED* defines it. The most recent example given, from 2007 in the *New York Times*, reflects concerns that are characteristic of current debates: 'Globalization should be managed by governments that represent their people and our planet, not by corporate empires that represent only their own short-term interests.'[1] While languages have spread with the migration of cultural groups throughout history, they also have an important part to play in the active 'making global' process – and in negotiating the tensions that arise from it.

National Identity and Globalization

The early modern period right through to the start of the twentieth century was an era of nation-building and imperial expansion, with European languages playing an important role in these processes. Spain and Portugal, England and France gained shape as cultural entities early on, and developed the political capability and naval power to expand globally. The enduringly Euro-centric perspective of that expansion is evident in the narrative of Christopher Columbus 'discovering' the 'New World' – two concepts that suggest the Americas were previously uninhabited and unknown to humankind. The omission of the indigenous peoples from the picture, masking brutal suppression and exploitation, is replicated in the partition of Africa that followed in the nineteenth and early twentieth century.

Conflict on an unprecedented global scale in two 'world wars' gradually led to correspondingly enhanced global cooperation. Learning from the failures of the toothless League of Nations founded after the First World War, a much stronger framework was developed for the United Nations, founded in 1945. It is a powerful, though constantly challenged force in global politics and social policy, working to maintain international peace and security, protect human rights, uphold international law, deliver human aid and promote sustainable development.[2] Global agendas also inform the work of complementary organizations founded in the twentieth century such as the World Health Organization (WHO), the World Trade Organization (WTO), the International Monetary Fund (IMF) and the World Bank. Languages play an important part in their global work: the UN has six official languages – Arabic, Chinese, English, French, Russian and Spanish – supported by highly ambitious translation and interpretation services.

The twenty-first century has seen both increasing nationalism and increasing globalization, with the two tendencies being mutually dependent. Religion has come to the fore as an important driver of tensions both within nations and in international conflict. Global migration has been fuelled by political destabilization in large regions such as the Middle East, and this has in turn put pressure on national borders, contributing to surges of nationalism. At the same time, globalization has become accepted as a fundamental feature of daily life in the form of electronic communication that is in principle capable of connecting up every home across the world with the 'World Wide Web'. It gives individuals the ability to communicate with others in different parts of the world without physical impediment – though as with all resources, access to them depends on economic and political factors.

The effects of globalization on individuals and whole nations became tangible with the Covid-19 pandemic, which spread inexorably across the world as a result of routine international travel. Its progress manifested itself differently depending on national policies and mentalities, living conditions and resources, with many national borders suddenly becoming impermeable as nations sought to control the spread. International cooperation played an important part as governments and medical teams pooled statistics, exchanged research findings concerning symptoms, tests and vaccines, and collaborated on equipment. Meanwhile national self-interest impacted on the global availability of medicines, vaccines and protective equipment. National isolation and international collaboration proved to be part of a single global phenomenon.

The early decades of the twenty-first century, then, have made people more aware of simultaneously being citizens of nations and citizens of the world. This same shift is also changing the subject of modern languages. Traditionally, there has been a tendency to equate the language being studied primarily with the nation state with which it is historically most obviously associated: for example, French with France, Spanish with Spain, Russian with Russia. Globalization has made it increasingly obvious that this model is too simplistic, and has its roots in a concept of linguistic identity that is informed by a one-sided focus on nationhood and a heritage of colonialism. More diverse, global perspectives have opened up ways of addressing these difficulties at the heart of the discipline by making them an explicit part of the subject, prompting far-reaching questions concerning the relationship between language and culture, society and nationhood, migration and colonialism.

Legacies of Colonialism

The European languages that have come to the fore as widely spoken 'world languages' or 'mega languages' have done so largely as a consequence of expansion into neighbouring territories – for example, by Germany and German-speaking parts of the Austro-Hungarian Empire into Central and Eastern Europe – or colonial expansion overseas, as with France, Great Britain, Portugal and Spain. Two examples will serve to illustrate the implications of those processes: the Codex Mendoza as a document of Spanish colonization of the Americas, and a cartoon in a late nineteenth-century French magazine depicting the 'carving up' of Africa.

The Codex Mendoza is a beautifully crafted manuscript created in 1541, twenty years after Hernán Cortés and his men conquered the Aztec city of Tenochtitlan in what is now Mexico City (see Figure 6). Its purpose was evidently to provide the Spanish authorities with information about the conquered Mexica people, and it consists of three parts: the first is a Mexica chronicle of victories; the second is a list of tributes paid by the peoples who had been conquered by the Aztecs; and the third provides details of Mexica cultural life. The manuscript is composed in Mexica picture writing

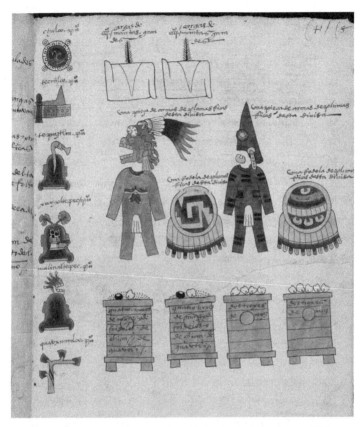

Figure 6. A page from the Codex Mendoza (1541). This part of the codex records the annual tribute the towns conquered by the Aztecs had to pay to their rulers in the city of Tenochtitlan, including warrior outfits and bins of beans and maize. (Bodleian Library MS. Arch. Selden. A. 1, folio 41r).

while also providing glosses in a newly created written form of the indigenous language Nahuatl, and in Spanish. The page facing the picture writing in each case offers translations into Spanish with interpretation woven in. The manuscript was destined for the court of Charles V but it was intercepted by pirates and ended up first in France and then in England, where it remains.

The codex gives a unique insight into a particular moment in the history of what is now Mexico. It provides anthropologically rich data about the peoples conquered by the Aztecs, a record of Aztec administration of conquered territories and a record of what the Aztecs documented for the Spaniards who were in the process of conquering them in turn. It also shows the importance of language and the processes of transliteration (i.e. converting oral language into writing), translation and interpretation in all their fluidity as one culture invades and appropriates another. Each pictorially depicted object of tribute allows us to imagine its practical and cultural meaningfulness for the people forced to deliver it to the Aztecs, a dimension that has meanwhile receded into history. However, through the Nahuatl language, Mexica culture has left traces in the Spanish language, especially in the variety of Spanish used in Mexico, providing names for indigenous plants, animals and foodstuffs, and also words for objects and materials for domestic use. Some words have indeed made it into English and global vocabulary, such as 'tomato', 'avocado', 'cacao/cocoa', 'chilli' and 'guacamole'.[3] We can see here how integral language is to cultural contact, often through trade, and to processes of cultural appropriation that may be violent or peaceful – or a complex mixture of both.

While it seems likely that the Codex Mendoza was produced by representatives of the conquered people in a strategic or forced collaboration with the conquering administration, the cartoon depicting the 'carving up' of Africa reflects the appropriation of an entire continent by the colonial powers in the course of the Berlin Conference of 1884–5 (see Figure 7). The straight cuts between the slices of the symbolic cake reflect the schematic way in which many of the borders were defined, without concern for established cultural entities or allegiances. Africa's political map continues to reflect the process by which the partition of Africa was implemented in the late nineteenth century and early twentieth century.

The list of nations participating in the conference gives a sense of the countries engaged in colonial occupation at that time. They included twelve

Figure 7. Unattributed cartoon published on 3 January 1885 in the French magazine *L'Illustration*, commenting on the Berlin Conference of 1884–5, which determined the colonial ownership of Africa. Otto von Bismarck, Chancellor of Germany and host of the conference, is wielding the knife.

Mary Evans Picture Library

European nations (Austria-Hungary, Belgium, Denmark, France, Germany, Great Britain, Italy, the Netherlands, Portugal, Russia, Spain and Sweden-Norway), the Ottoman Empire (centred on its capital Constantinople, now Istanbul) and the United States. No African leaders were invited. Exacerbating the detrimental effects of the previous colonial free-for-all, the conference laid the basis for the catastrophic exploitation of Africa that continues today.

Much as the modern linguistic map of the Americas reflects the European powers involved in colonizing the continent from the fifteenth century onwards, today's linguistic map of Africa reflects the dominant players in the historical race for colonial control of the continent. While Great Britain occupied territories along the entire stretch of some 10,000 km from Cairo to the Cape of Good Hope, France took control of much of western and central Africa and many islands – a territory overall that was some ten times as big as France itself.

The linguistic map is, however, complex and multi-layered, for the official or dominant languages of the erstwhile respective colonial territories are only part of the picture. They constitute lingua francas established by the respective administrations, and in each case, the language of the erstwhile colonial power continues to facilitate communication across local cultural groups within the country, between African countries, and with other continents. Alongside and in interaction with those European lingua francas, people use indigenous lingua francas, more local languages and creoles.

Take a person living in Dakar, capital of Senegal. Their first or second language will normally be Wolof, the main lingua franca of that part of West Africa. Meanwhile the official language of Senegal is French, the administrative lingua franca established under colonial rule in what was until 1958 French West Africa. It is the main language of instruction in schools as well as the main written language, but it tends to be confined to the social elite, being understood by only around one fifth of men in Senegal and a tiny fraction of the female population. In homes, the main language will often be one of the many local Senegalese languages such as Pulaar, Seereer or Joola. Deaf people may learn American Sign Language. The dominant Muslim faith gives classical Arabic a role in people's lives, though mainly receptively at places of worship and maybe Qur'anic school. Meanwhile, for people involved in the tourist industry, international business or in the sciences, and also for local traders, English has become a crucial lingua franca alongside French.

The example of Senegal shows that in many parts of the world, the language or languages a person speaks will depend on a multitude of different factors pertaining to different aspects of their life, and the constellation of languages spoken by the people they interact with. A language can connect us to many networks that may in turn overlap. Correspondingly, learning a language gives us more than a new linguistic medium. It connects us into many new networks of human intercourse and opens up a new and multi-faceted cultural perspective on the world.

Modern languages emerged as a discipline out of the contexts of colonial empire, a context that only began to be subjected to scrutiny towards the end of the twentieth century. An objective of twenty-first-century syllabus reforms in modern languages departments is to 'decolonize' and 'transnationalize' the syllabus by uncoupling languages from national definitions, opening up the cultural topics studied, embracing ethnic minorities and bringing voices into the foreground that go beyond the traditional canon. A key project is to address rather than simply confirm colonial hierarchies, and make modern languages a force that challenges the ongoing influences of cultural imperialism.

There is, however, an inescapable tension built into seeking to decolonize a subject that is to a considerable extent defined by hierarchies which have their roots in colonialism. The study of modern languages needs to take account of that tension, and it also matters where the subject is being studied. The answer does not lie in abandoning the study of languages that have an ethically problematic history – in anglophone contexts, the result would be to further empower English – or to substitute generic overviews of language constellations for in-depth learning of one or more particular languages. Rather, the way forward lies in pursuing the study of particular languages, on which the study of further languages can be based, and in studying languages not as disembodied tools of transactional communication but in their messy interconnections with their cultural and political histories and contexts. This can go some way towards ensuring that modern linguists are equipped to understand cultural difference and the implications of cultural and linguistic hierarchies. It should also entail taking active responsibility for giving agency, and a voice, to groups whose voices are suppressed by mutually reinforcing political, cultural and linguistic disempowerment. In our globalized world, that work can start right where we find ourselves – in our own multilingual countries and local communities.

National or Transnational?

Languages are often represented by national flags – an iconic shorthand for an apparently obvious connection between a language and the culture in which it is embedded. However, such a connection takes no account of the complexities discussed above that govern the relationship between languages and nation states. As a cultural phenomenon, language identity is not just political. Indeed, cultural groups may be at odds with national entities, and they may extend across national borders. Such tensions can promote transnational migration, as can the desire or need for an individual, family or group to seek a livelihood beyond their home country. Cultural and linguistic diasporas – communities that have migrated and established themselves in other parts of the world – are part of the subject of modern languages.

The varied ways in which the relationship between language and nation may play out is evident in the four languages with the largest numbers of speakers in the world (calculated both in terms of first-language speakers and in terms of the estimated total number of speakers):[4]

Mandarin Chinese is the language with by far the largest number of first-language speakers in the world. It is relatively concentrated geographically, being spoken in China, some neighbouring countries and Singapore, but there are also large Chinese communities in other parts of the world. There are eight main varieties of speech in China, and while these are often referred to as dialects, differences among spoken variants of Chinese are in some cases and respects even greater than differences between, for example, Spanish and Italian. China is currently engaged in 'the most ambitious programme of language planning the world has ever seen', designed to establish Beijing-based Mandarin as a standard spoken language for the whole of China and simplify the writing system.[5]

Spanish has the second largest number of first-language speakers. It is the main official language of Spain and of countries right across Central and South America, with Mexico alone having more than twice as many first-language Spanish speakers as Spain. The number of people in the United States speaking Spanish as their first language – mainly in the states closest to Mexico – is likely to be roughly equal to the population of Spain.

English spoken as a first language is geographically and nationally highly dispersed. It is the first and often only language of most people in the United States and Canada, the United Kingdom and Ireland, Australia and New Zealand. It is also the main language, or the main lingua franca, in many countries of Africa, and an official language of India and Pakistan. It is the most widely spoken language in the world if speakers of English beyond first-language speakers are factored in.

Hindi is spoken across northern and central India. While there have been moves to establish it as the sole official language of India, it has little presence in southern India and is often rejected there, with speakers of Indian languages other than Hindi often supporting the retention of English as an alternative official language. Hindi is more widely spoken globally than Spanish if speakers beyond first-language competence are factored in. Moreover, there is an argument for including speakers of *Urdu*, which is the official language of Pakistan alongside English. Hindi and Urdu are to a large extent mutually intelligible and could be considered as two dialects of the same language, though with distinct writing systems. However, while Mahatma Gandhi proposed establishing a common language called 'Hindustani', religious and political division promoted differentiation.

Language will always be an important issue for a nation, since it constitutes a significant aspect of its internal identity, organization and control, and shapes its relationship with the rest of the world. Understanding how a language relates to the nations and cultural groups that use it is a key area of study in modern languages – one that will always need to be specific and sensitive to difference, though understanding the forces prevailing in one context will sharpen awareness that is transferable to others. Equally important is understanding the forces that work across boundaries and the mechanisms that enable transnational activity to happen. Such activity has grown more prominent in the era of globalization. It can be studied with respect to all areas of cultural life, from diplomatic relations and business through world literature to transnational pop culture.

One of the most obvious areas of transcultural and transnational movement has always been trade, and the World Trade Organization's definition of its negotiatory work provides an illuminating model of the complex interplay between national and transnational forces: 'Where countries have faced trade barriers and wanted them lowered, the negotiations have helped to open markets for trade. But [. . .] in some circumstances its rules support maintaining trade barriers – for example, to protect consumers or prevent the spread of disease.'[6] The 'barriers' in question consist of virtual administrative structures, and they are constructed or dismantled by means of verbal communication.

Such virtual barriers and border crossings are intrinsic to globalization processes in all areas of cultural activity. This is particularly evident in the development of the internet: for example, in the erection of 'firewalls' that serve to control both incoming and outgoing traffic. They can be used to establish sovereignty and implement censorship. Interaction with language is obvious where there is a state policy of exerting control by means of a nationally controlled, language-specific internet. For example, what has become known as the 'Great Firewall of China' restricts internet access for citizens of the People's Republic of China to sole use of the Chinese internet. Meanwhile, Vladimir Putin's regime has placed increasing importance on developing the Russian-language internet, or Runet, as a means of controlling access to content.[7]

Beyond such nationally specific political barriers, a multitude of mechanisms determine what is accessed by individuals, with language playing an important part in the process of filtering and directing content. Neither Chinese people nor Russians uniformly share the view that the Chinese internet and the Runet respectively are more ideologically controlled than the internet that is accessible via Google. In order to compare systems, it is necessary to have cross-linguistic and cross-cultural competence. Moreover, that competence needs to be widely distributed so that a maximally wide range of cultural and political perspectives can inform the debate.

Ultimately, the World Wide Web is proving less barrier-free than it seems, and 'global English' is not as ubiquitous as it appears to English-speaking users. Even in this most virtual medium of communication, language diversity needs to be attended to and its significance understood in relation to cultural diversity.

Empowering Language Diversity

This book is written in English, and is addressed most obviously to English-speaking readers. As 'global English' has extended its reach in all areas of public, social and private life, and increasingly through electronic media, speakers of English as their first language have acquired an exposed role to fulfil in embracing, respecting and working to strengthen language diversity. This is not just optional, and it is not just a matter that is relevant to people who happen to have an interest in languages or language learning. Language diversity is a human rights issue.

A basis for recognizing a community's right to speak and maintain its language without suffering discrimination was already established in the four main purposes of the United Nations enshrined in its Charter. One of those is achieving international cooperation in 'promoting and encouraging respect for human rights and for fundamental freedoms for all without distinction as to race, sex, language, or religion'.[8] However, eliminating discrimination on grounds of language holds particular challenges. This is because asserting any right depends on making oneself heard in a language that is shared by those in power. Minority cultural groups are often linguistically marginalized as well, as is evident in the huge power imbalance between the groups who speak a language empowered by imperial expansion and those who speak – or spoke – a language suppressed or obliterated by such expansion.

Taking account of language diversity is relevant to every one of the seventeen Sustainable Development Goals adopted by the UN in 2015, which include 'No Poverty', 'Good Health and Well-Being',

'Quality Education', 'Gender Equality', 'Industry, Innovation, and Infrastructure', 'Climate Action', 'Life Below Water' and 'Life On Land'.[9] Factoring in language diversity is vital in order to ensure that people belonging to linguistic minorities have access to the information, opportunities and support that are necessary for achieving the goals, and that they are able to make their voice heard.

Action is required in three directions. Firstly, minority languages need to be protected in order to enable their speakers to express themselves, gain education in the language they best understand, and communicate their local knowledge in the language that has developed in interaction with the local cultural and biological context. This requires education in the local language. Secondly, speakers of minority languages need to be educated in a lingua franca and translation skills, so that they can mediate effectively between their local language and a language that enables them to take part in global dialogues. Thirdly, speakers of widely dispersed lingua francas – and currently especially speakers of English as their first language – need to be educated to understand and respect the importance of linguistic diversity and language learning.

According to UNESCO – the UN's Educational, Scientific and Cultural Organization – 40% of the global population does not access education in a language they understand.[10] This in turn exacerbates all other kinds of inequality. For example, the UN's stated goal of improving women's 'representation in political and economic decision-making processes' – part of the Gender Equality goal – depends on their gaining competence, initially through their first language, in a language that is used for such decision-making processes. Healthcare, including acceptance of vaccination, similarly depends on effective communication in a language understood by the patient, with the Covid-19 pandemic having highlighted that taking full account of linguistic diversity is crucial for equal access to information and health provision.[11] Providing access to industry, innovation and infrastructure, and involving indigenous people in planning and delivery, depend on functioning dialogue that takes full account of local knowledge. And in order to involve indigenous people in climate action and effective management and conservation of resources below water and on land, it is vital to facilitate effective communication that fully involves local knowledge – and that means cultural knowledge vested in local languages. The UN's Sustainable Development Goals open up the big context from which the discipline of modern languages gains its significance.

Most modern linguists will study only one or two languages, usually a language that has relatively wide distribution, with all the advantages and dangers that entails. Each one will be complex in the present with a multifaceted past. And there will always be tremendous cultural riches to be discovered. Close engagement with a language, the cultural contexts it interacts with and the works of art in which it gains consummate expression is, however, valuable far beyond the expertise it provides in that language and those cultures. It trains our multilingual capabilities, sensitizes us to linguistic and cultural difference, and develops our understanding of the vital role languages play in shaping, and giving expression to, the diversity of cultural identities that is fundamental to humankind. By learning one language in depth, we equip ourselves to learn others. Moreover, we strengthen our ability to value other cultures, and gain experience in understanding new worlds of thought, creative expression and cultural practice.

Afterword: Sustaining a Multilingual Future

Languages facilitate communication across groups, and distinguish one cultural group from another. Both functions are built into human communication. The fact that babies already start learning to recognize language difference before they are born (see Chapter 1) indicates how vital the distinctiveness of our language must be for our personal interaction with the society on which our survival and mental health depends. It also shows that a language is much more than a useful tool for getting things done. It is integrated with the culture it forms part of, as a defining force and its most fundamental medium of expression.

Studying modern languages demands intense engagement with the interaction between language and culture both in practice and in theory. This develops a high level of expertise in the language or languages being studied, in the cultural contexts with which they are associated, and in the ways in which language and culture intersect. It also lays a strong foundation for taking the study of languages further, enriched by a deep understanding of the multifaceted ways in which they are embedded in culture and contribute to it.

Languages will continue to exist as diverse forms of communication for as long as human beings do. But that diversity can be rich, inclusive and enabling, or it can become impoverished and serve as a means of excluding or suppressing minorities. Sustaining a healthy diversity of languages, and giving cultural groups the scope both to use and develop their languages and contribute through them to the global conversation, is one of the great issues of our time. Given the current role of English as the most widely used lingua franca, speakers of English as their first language are particularly challenged when it comes to appreciating the nature and value of linguistic diversity. At the same time, they have a particular responsibility to respect, embrace and promote it. For much like uncontrolled business interests are threatening biodiversity, the domination of English is threatening linguistic diversity. This has considerable negative knock-on effects for diversity in the sciences, social sciences and humanities, for inclusive business and trade, for participation especially of women in global public life, and for education in non-anglophone countries.

The recent addition of a new word to the *Oxford English Dictionary* gives a glimpse of the impact the colonial legacy can continue to have in the current world. The word 'Anglosphere' – coined in 1995 in a sci-fi novel – was included in June 2020 with the definition 'English-speaking countries considered collectively; *esp.* the United Kingdom, the United States, Canada, Australia, and New Zealand (and sometimes other countries), regarded as a group with a shared historical and cultural heritage'.[1] The Wikipedia definition goes further in referring to 'close political, diplomatic and military cooperation' among the countries involved.[2] A shared language here serves as a means of asserting a shared historical and cultural heritage – a heritage that is grounded in colonialism. A key question raised by the word is how the asserted shared heritage relates to the distinctive heritages of the individual countries involved, and the participation of indigenous peoples and their languages in the heritages of those English-speaking nations. The concept of English that is embedded in the word 'Anglosphere' refers not just to a shared lingua franca but also to a force that obliterates local historical, cultural and linguistic difference.

For speakers of languages other than English, the principle that lingua francas should interact with local languages is readily understood, though cultural or national pride may fuel the urge to establish cultural independence by strengthening a linguistic identity that is distinct from English even if knowledge of English is widespread. By contrast, speakers of English as their first and only language need to learn the very principle, pleasure and political force of linguistic diversity. The rewards are great, for learning a language becomes tantamount to understanding a fundamental aspect of human culture and what it means to be human. It opens up a unique pathway to appreciating the value of languages – in the plural – as a fundamental human freedom.

Globalization has not done away with the need for modern linguists – if anything, they are more necessary than ever. We need people who can speak more than one language, who find cultural diversity stimulating rather than threatening, and who are able to draw on the rich resources of emotional and cultural intelligence as well as creative imagination that the study of modern languages fosters. In all walks of life – from law and commerce to health, education and the creative arts – it is essential to have people who are curious about language diversity as expressing and sustaining cultural diversity. There is a need for people who have the mental and cultural agility to interpret rather than judge differences, and for people who want to facilitate cross-cultural dialogue. If such dialogue is to work effectively, sustaining language difference is as important as sharing languages.

Notes

Chapter 1 Understanding Identity

1 This estimate follows John C. Maher, *Multilingualism: A Very Short Introduction* (Oxford: Oxford University Press, 2017), p. 7. The web-based catalogue *Ethnologue.com* identifies 7,117 languages in its 23rd edition (2020). For a discussion of the criteria, and a more conservative estimate of around 6,000 languages, see David Crystal, *The Cambridge Encyclopedia of Language*, 3rd edn (Cambridge: Cambridge University Press, 2010), p. 295.

2 See Albert Costa, *The Bilingual Brain: And What It Tells Us about the Science of Language*, trans. John W. Schwieter (London: Allen Lane, 2019), pp. 14f.

3 'Facebook scraps A.I. chatbots after they created their own language', *https://www.youtube.com/watch?v=ONPqeHJShdQ*.

4 See the following studies: Ricardo Antunes et al., 'Individually distinctive acoustic features in sperm

whale codas', *Animal Behaviour* 81(4) (2011): 723–30; Andy Coghlan, 'Young goats can develop distinct accents', *New Scientist*, 16 February 2012, *https://www.newscientist.com/article/dn21481-young -goats-can-develop-distinct-accents*; Pavel Pipek et al., 'Dialects of an invasive songbird are preserved in its invaded but not native source range', *Ecography* 41 (2018): 245–54.

5 Margaret Atwood et al., 'Reconnecting kids with nature is vital, and needs cultural leadership', Letter to the Oxford University Press, 2015, *http://www. naturemusicpoetry.com/uploads/2/9/3/8/29384149/ letter_to_oup_final.pdf*.

6 See Alan Kirkness, Peter Kühn and Herbert Ernst Wiegand (eds), *Studien zum Deutschen Wörterbuch von Jacob Grimm und Wilhelm Grimm*, vol. 1 (Tübingen: Niemeyer, 1991), p. 365.

7 See 'L'Académie française contre les langues régio-nales dans la Constitution', *Libération*, 17 June 2008, *https://www.liberation.fr/societe/2008/06/17/l-acade mie-francaise-contre-les-langues-regionales-dans-la-constitution_21244*.

8 Alison Phipps makes the case for radical decoloniza-tion of academic practice with respect to languages in *Decolonising Multilingualism: Struggles to Decreate* (Bristol: Multilingual Matters, 2019).

9 For the US figures, see the report *America's Languages: Investing in Language Education for the 21st Century* by the American Academy of Arts & Sciences (Cambridge, Mass., 2017), p. 4, *https://www. amacad.org/sites/default/files/publication/down*

*loads/Commission-on-Language-Learning_Ameri
cas-Languages.pdf.*

Chapter 2 Experimenting with a New Medium

1 *https://www.youtube.com/watch?v=OJF7UQGK5
   tg.*
2 David Crystal, *Language Play* (London: Penguin,
   1998).
3 Project MEITS, Heather Martin and Wendy Ayres-
   Bennett (eds), *How Languages Changed My Life*
   ([n. p.]: Archway, 2019). See also the following series
   of videos: Creative Multilingualism, *How Languages
   Help in Your Career*, *https://www.creativeml.ox.ac.
   uk/careers*.
4 Jhumpa Lahiri, *In Other Words*, with a translation
   by Ann Goldstein (London: Bloomsbury, 2017).
5 See the book and videos given in note 3.
6 There are no reliable data on the number of bilingual and multilingual people in the world, not least
   because population census data do not generally
   record how many languages a citizen speaks. For
   a summary of the evidence, see Tej K. Bhatia and
   William C. Ritchie, *The Handbook of Bilingualism
   and Multilingualism*, 2nd edn (Malden, Mass., and
   Oxford: Blackwell, 2014), p. xxi. For a discussion
   of historical evidence, see Nicholas Evans, 'Did language evolve in multilingual settings?', *Biology &
   Philosophy* 32 (2017): 905–33.
7 See Costa, *The Bilingual Brain*, pp. 112–20 for a discussion of the field around 2017 (when the original

Spanish edition was published). See also the studies conducted by Thomas H. Bak and other information listed on the website of the Healthy Linguistic Diet project by Bak and Dina Mehmedbegovic: *www.healthylinguisticdiet.com*. Still the most thorough study in this field is Suvarna Alladi et al., 'Bilingualism delays age at onset of dementia independent of education and immigration status', *Neurology* 81(22) (2013), doi: 10.1212/01.wnl.0000436620.33155.a4.

8 Wolfgang Klein, *Second Language Acquisition* (Cambridge: Cambridge University Press, 1986), p. 9.

9 See the website *Global Graduates* for advice and personal stories concerning the year abroad and more generally spending periods working or studying abroad: *https://globalgraduates.com/*.

Chapter 3 Exploring Difference

1 Johann Wolfgang Goethe, *Sämtliche Werke, Briefe, Tagebücher und Gespräche*, vol. 13: *Sprüche in Prosa. Sämtliche Maximen und Reflexionen*, ed. Harald Fricke (Frankfurt a. M.: Deutscher Klassiker Verlag, 1993), p. 12.

2 See Costa, *The Bilingual Brain*, pp. 97–109, esp. pp. 99–101.

3 Umberto Eco, *Mouse or Rat? Translation as Negotiation* (London: Phoenix, 2004), p. 82. The book is based on a series of lectures given in English.

4 For the meaning of the Hebrew, see Francis Brown,

S.R. Driver and Charles A. Briggs, *A Hebrew and English Lexicon of the Old Testament [. . .]* (Boston: Riverside, 1906), p. 697. Luther's translation of the verse is discussed in Walter Jens, 'Martin Luther: Die Deutsche Bibel einst und jetzt', in Jens, *Ort der Handlung ist Deutschland: Reden in erinnerungsfeindlicher Zeit* (Munich: Kindler, 1981), pp. 147–64 (p. 152). For North American and British editions of *The Living Bible* see, respectively, Kenneth N. Taylor, *The Living Bible, Paraphrased* (Wheaton, Ill.: Tyndale House, [1971]), and Kenneth N. Taylor, *The Living Bible* (London: Coverdale House, Hodder & Stoughton, 1974).

Chapter 4 Training Cultural Intelligence

1 See P. Christopher Earley and Soon Ang, *Cultural Intelligence: Individual Interactions across Cultures* (Stanford, Calif.: Stanford University Press, 2003).
2 Benjamin Lee Whorf, 'Science and linguistics', in *Language, Thought, and Reality: Selected Writings of Benjamin Lee Whorf*, ed. John B. Carroll (Cambridge, Mass.: MIT Press, 1964), pp. 207–19 (p. 214).
3 See for example Geoffrey K. Pullum, 'The great Eskimo vocabulary hoax', in Pullum, *The Great Eskimo Vocabulary Hoax and Other Irreverent Essays on the Study of Language* (Chicago and London: University of Chicago Press, 1991), pp. 159–71.
4 See Lera Boroditsky, 'How languages construct time',

in Stanislas Dehaene and Elizabeth Brannon (eds), *Space, Time and Number in the Brain: Searching for the Foundations of Mathematical Thought* (London: Elsevier, 2011), pp. 333–41. For a discussion of the role of metaphor at the interface between cognition and language, see Katrin Kohl, Marianna Bolognesi and Ana Werkmann Horvat, 'The creative power of metaphor', in Katrin Kohl et al. (eds), *Creative Multilingualism: A Manifesto* (Cambridge: Open Book, 2020), pp. 25–46.

5 Ben Panko, 'English is the language of science. That isn't always a good thing', *Smithsonian Magazine*, 2 January 2017, *https://www.smithsonianmag.com/ science-nature/english-language-science-can-cause-pr oblems-180961623/.*

6 UNEP, 'Global Environment Outlook 4: Environment for Development' (Nairobi: UNEP, 2007), p. 160, *https://www.unenvironment.org/resources/global- environment-outlook-4.* See also Karen Park et al., 'Creating a meaningful world: nature in name, metaphor, and myth', in Kohl et al. (eds), *Creative Multilingualism,* pp. 47–68.

7 Marek Kohn, 'Using more than one language matters now more than ever', *The Big Issue,* 11 February 2020, *https://www.bigissue.com/culture/books/us ing-more-than-one-language-matters-now-more-than -ever/.*

8 James Foreman-Peck and Yi Wang, 'The costs to the UK of language deficiencies as a barrier to UK engagement in exporting: a report to UK Trade & Investment' (Cardiff: Cardiff Business School, 2014),

p. 35, *https://assets.publishing.service.gov.uk/gov ernment/uploads/system/uploads/attachment_data/ file/309899/Costs_to_UK_of_language_deficien cies_as_barrier_to_UK_engagement_in_exporting. pdf.*

9 McElroy Translation [now TranslateMedia], 'Funny but costly translation mistakes', *https://www.transla tiondirectory.com/articles/article2409.php.*

10 *The Japan Times*, 'Hong Kong gamers gripe over Nintendo's shift to Mandarin-based names for Pokémon characters', 1 June 2016, *https://www. japantimes.co.jp/news/2016/06/01/national/hong-kong-gamers-gripe-nintendos-shift-mandarin-based-names-pokemon-characters/#.Xn0grIj7RPY.*

11 BBC, 'Why the plan to rename Pikachu has made Hong Kong angry', 31 May 2016, *https://www.bbc. co.uk/news/world-asia-china-36414978.*

12 See Crystal, *The Cambridge Encyclopedia of Language*, p. 322.

13 Earley and Ang, *Cultural Intelligence*, p. 11.

Chapter 5 Developing the Imagination

1 Stromae, 'Alors on danse', TEDxBrussels, *https:// www.youtube.com/watch?v=iDGvWX-tFGM.*

2 *https://www.youtube.com/watch?list=PLW9Nsm1H JiIvFVz27gS4UAJ0F7l8BeryT&v=oiKj0Z_Xnjc.*

3 Rosalía has commented on the connection between the album and the medieval romance in various con-texts: see, e.g., Ecleen Luzmila Caraballo, 'Rosalía is redefining flamenco', *Jezebel*, 2 November 2018,

https://themuse.jezebel.com/rosalia-is-redefining-fla menco-1830164344. *The Romance of Flamenca*, ed. and trans. E.D. Blodgett (Abingdon: Routledge, 1995); see also Sarah Kay, 'Flamenca', in Peter France (ed.), *The New Oxford Companion to Literature in French* (Oxford: Oxford University Press, 1995), p. 314.

4 *https://www.youtube.com/watch?v=cENIOFk160c*.

5 *https://www.youtube.com/watch?v=Rht7rBHuXW8*.

6 Álvaro Piñero 'The ultimate guide to understanding Rosalía's references', *i-D*, 19 August 2019, *https://i d. vice.com/en_uk/article/9kx47y/guide-to-rosalia-lyrics-references*; TheUrbanEve, 'Explaining Rosalía's "Pienso en tu mirá" in English', 16 April 2019, *https://www.youtube.com/watch?v=JO7qFDu65Rg*.

7 See Alvaro Arroba and Fernando Ganzo, 'Almodóvar: sa grande confession', *Sofilm,* 9 May 2016, *http:// www.sofilm.fr/almodovar-sa-grande-confession*.

8 Ibid.

9 Franz Kafka, *Die Verwandlung*, in Kafka, *Die Erzählungen und andere ausgewählte Prosa*, ed. Roger Hermes (Frankfurt/M.: Fischer, 1996), pp. 96–161 (p. 96). Franz Kafka, *Metamorphosis*, in Kafka, *Metamorphosis and Other Stories*, trans. Michael Hofmann (London: Penguin, 2015), pp. 73–126 (p. 75).

10 Albert Camus, *La Peste* (Paris: Gallimard, 1947), p. 5; Albert Camus, *The Plague*, trans. Stuart Gilbert (London: Penguin, 2010), p. 1.

11 *La Peste*, p. 6; *The Plague*, p. 2.

12 *La Peste* , p. 34; *The Plague*, p. 36.

13 *La Peste* , p. 107, see also p. 55; *The Plague*, p. 120, see also p. 60.

14 *La Peste* , pp. 67f.; *The Plague*, p. 74.

15 *La Peste*, p. 5; the Defoe quotation is omitted from this translation. It is from the third book featuring Robinson Crusoe: Daniel Defoe, *Serious Reflections during the Life and Surprising Adventures of Robinson Crusoe [...]. Written by Himself* (London: W. Taylor, 1720), Preface (unpaginated).

16 See Margaret E. Gray, 'Layers of meaning in *La Peste*', in Edward Hughes (ed.), *The Cambridge Companion to Camus* (Cambridge: Cambridge University Press, 2007), pp. 165–77.

17 *La Peste*, p. 255; *The Plague*, p. 297.

Chapter 6 Negotiating Globalization

1 'globalization, *n.*', in *Oxford English Dictionary*, *https://www.oed.com/view/Entry/272264?redirected From=globalization#eid*.

2 United Nations, 'What we do', *https://www.un.org/ en/sections/what-we-do/index.html*.

3 Further words can be found on websites such as *https://en.wikipedia.org/wiki/List_of_English_words _from_indigenous_languages_of_the_Americas*.

4 Figures and rankings vary since criteria diverge, and languages are continuously on the move. Establishing statistically reliable data is notoriously difficult even at national level. There is, however, largely a consensus on the four most widely spoken languages. See *https://www.ethnologue.com/guides/*

most-spoken-languages and *https://www.ethno-logue.com/guides/ethnologue200*.

5 Crystal, *The Cambridge Encyclopedia of Language*, p. 322.

6 World Trade Organization, 'Who we are', *https://www.wto.org/english/thewto_e/whatis_e/who_we_are_e.htm*.

7 See Michael Gorham, 'Beyond a world with one master: the rhetorical dimensions of Putin's "sovereign internet"', in Andy Byford, Connor Doak and Stephen Hutchings (eds), *Transnational Russian Studies* (Liverpool: Liverpool University Press, 2020), pp. 266–82.

8 Article 1 of the Charter of the United Nations, setting out the purposes of the United Nations, *https://www.un.org/en/sections/un-charter/chapter-i/index.html*.

9 See the outline of the UN's Sustainable Development Goals, *https://www.un.org/sustainabledevelopment/sustainable-development-goals/*.

10 See the summary of the UNESCO report 'If you don't understand, how can you learn?' (2016) and the link to the full report, *https://en.unesco.org/news/40-don-t-access-education-language-they-understand*. See also the British Council article by Angelina Kioko, 'Why schools should teach learners in home languages', *Voices Magazine*, 16 January 2015, *https://www.britishcouncil.org/voices-magazine/why-schools-should-teach-young-learners-home-language*.

11 See Perspective #2 from Ingrid Piller in '12 perspectives on the pandemic: social science thought leaders reflect on Covid-19', *https://www.degruyter.com/*

fileasset/craft/media/doc/DG_12perspectives_social-sciences.pdf.

Afterword: Sustaining a Multilingual Future

1 'Anglosphere, n.', in *Oxford English Dictionary*, *https://www.oed.com/view/Entry/84268234.*
2 'Anglosphere', definition accessed on 4 July 2020, *https://en.wikipedia.org/wiki/Anglosphere.*

Further Reading

The discipline of modern languages explores the interaction between languages and cultures, and it is grounded in diversity. The choice of language or languages, and the cultural focus, will open up specific fields of study and determine what reading is most relevant. The following suggestions focus on books and resources that address areas of overarching interest.

David Crystal, *The Cambridge Encyclopedia of Language*, 3rd edn (Cambridge: Cambridge University Press, 2010).

This large volume is a treasure trove of highly readable articles that illuminate innumerable aspects of language and language diversity.

Further Reading

Ethnologue: Languages of the World, *https://www.eth nologue.com/*.

An annually updated resource that offers the most comprehensive source of information on the world's living languages. It is published in the United States by the Christian faith-based organization SIL International, with a missionary purpose, though the services are provided 'without regard to religious belief, political ideology, gender, race or ethnic background' (*https:// www.sil.org/about*).

Albert Costa, *The Bilingual Brain: And What It Tells Us about the Science of Language*, trans. from Spanish by John W. Schwieter (London: Allen Lane, 2019).

An accessible account of neuropsychological research on bilingualism, including discussion of such areas as language development, the role of accent in our perception of other people, and ways in which bilingualism affects decision-making and conflict resolution.

John C. Maher, *Multilingualism: A Very Short Introduction* (Oxford: Oxford University Press, 2017).

This introduction to a complex topic enables the reader to appreciate the rich multitude of languages, dialects and styles in human communication, and the continuous traffic between languages.

Further Reading

Katrin Kohl et al. (eds), *Creative Multilingualism: A Manifesto* (Cambridge: Open Book Publishers, 2020).

This book makes the case for seeing language diversity and creativity as mutually enriching, looking at areas such as cognition, biocultural diversity, performative arts, literature and invented languages. Chapter 3 explores how relationships between languages can help with vocabulary learning.

Edward Said, *Orientalism* [1978] (London: Penguin, 2003).

A seminal work that changed cultural perspectives and opened up the field of postcolonial studies. Together with the prefaces in current editions, it remains a thought-provoking read.

Alison Phipps, *Decolonising Multilingualism: Struggles to Decreate* (Bristol: Multilingual Matters, 2019).

An experimental book that addresses the challenge of decolonizing syllabuses and attitudes, not just in what it says but also in its form. It offers deeply personal perspectives on decolonizing the body, decolonizing the heart and decolonizing the mind, with languages playing a central role throughout.

Transnational Modern Languages (Liverpool: Liverpool University Press, 2020–).

Further Reading

The Transnational Modern Languages series examines the discipline of modern languages as the study of languages, cultures and their interactions. The series includes a handbook, and volumes for French, German, Italian, Portuguese, Russian and Spanish.

Ben Hutchinson, *Comparative Literature: A Very Short Introduction* (Oxford: Oxford University Press, 2018).

An invitation to discover how literatures written in different languages interact across cultures and across time.

Marina Warner, *Once Upon a Time: A Short History of Fairy Tale* (Oxford: Oxford University Press, 2016).

An exploration of fairy tales and their travels across traditions, offering rich insights into the love of storytelling that is shared across cultures, and ways in which enduring motifs change in the course of transmission.

Matthew Reynolds, *Translation: A Very Short Introduction* (Oxford: Oxford University Press, 2016).

A wide-ranging introduction to key questions in translation that shows how fluid movement across languages opens up new meanings.

Umberto Eco, *Mouse or Rat? Translation as Negotiation* (London: Phoenix, 2004).

An engaging discussion of translation in practice, with a wealth of fascinating examples, from the author of the historical murder mystery *The Name of the Rose*.

Project MEITS, Heather Martin and Wendy Ayres-Bennett (eds), *How Languages Changed My Life* ([n. p.]: Archway, 2019).

A collection of autobiographical stories that offer insights into the transformative role that languages – over forty in all – have had for individuals in many different types of career.

Creative Multilingualism, *How Languages Help in Your Career, https://www.creativeml.ox.ac.uk/careers*.

A short film consisting of interviews with people in a variety of careers talking about the part languages play in their work. The full interviews are also provided in the form of separate videos.

Index

Index

Index

Index

Index

Index

Index

Index

Index

Index

Index

Index

Index

Index